Living on the Edge of Heaven

Living on the Edge of Heaven

(Sharing a moment each day with me)

———◆———

Author: I AM

A Daily Inspirational Devotional Prayer Book for All Believers in Christ

Compiled from the private prayer life of Joseph Bartkow (Sub-Author)

XULON PRESS

Xulon Press
2301 Lucien Way #415
Maitland, FL 32751
407.339.4217
www.xulonpress.com

© 2020 by I AM

All rights reserved solely by the author. The author guarantees all contents are original and do not infringe upon the legal rights of any other person or work. No part of this book may be reproduced in any form without the permission of the author. The views expressed in this book are not necessarily those of the publisher.

Printed in the United States of America.

Paperback ISBN-13: 978-1-6322-1302-0
eBook ISBN-13: 978-1-6322-1303-7

Welcome Letter to Readers

Many of God's children may be unfamiliar with the Father's goodness; how kind, gentle and loving He truly is. This book may be an avenue to a new beginning shared with The Father and His Son to reveal His love for ALL his children.

May what you receive each day be planted in your heart forever.

God bless you and His Son in your life forever.

Joe Bartkow

Living on the Edge of Heaven
(Sharing a moment each day with me)

———◆———

<u>Heavenly Father,</u> You have always overwhelmed me with unselfish love and gifts. In return my Lord, I want to share straight from my heart what is pleasing to You What shall You ask in this day of thee?

<u>My child,</u> your time. This time each day spent alone with Me in prayer. The Father and I want to instruct you, teach you, counsel you and share Our thoughts with you.
What you receive in your spirit my child,
"Let it be shared with many."

<u>Lord,</u> open the door of this heart to receive Your thoughts and will gratefully.
Guide me on this blessed day to share all You have spoken with love, joy and with each other.

I ask and pray in Jesus precious name,
AMEN

Father, in my success in life, help me to remember who I am,

A child of Yours
A believer in Your word
A worshipper of Your name
And a disciple of Yours forever.

Thank You, Jesus, for all
Amen!

To All My Brothers and Sisters in "Christ"

I want you all to know how blessed I am to share with those who share their beliefs in Jesus Christ as our Lord and Savior.

God through His Son Jesus has shared His heart with me in my spirit with these messages to share with others.

Each morning as He spoke and I listened, chills ran through me like cold water in a hot shower.

How could I not share with others His heart touching thoughts that came from our Lord and Savior.

May God bless you and your family with what you are about to read.

Your brother in Christ,
Joe Bartkow

About the Author

What my brothers and sisters in Christ are about to read are <u>inspirational messages</u> from the father's heart.

Each morning I start with prayers to the Father full of thankfulness of His goodness, mercy, grace and how much love He has placed in my heart.

It all started in the spring of 2013 while praying and listening, a voice spoke into my heart. First thought of mine was a misunderstanding about where this message was forming from.

A repetition of each message was being spoken. How unfamiliar my praying and hearing became; a different message each day, sometimes more than one in the same day.

I began to record them daily on a notepad. By April 2019, I was unsure if they were leading me any place. Over 1500 messages were recorded.

Sometime in mid May 2019, as I was praying,
I heard God repeat this message in my spirit:

<u>Share Me with ALL My children</u>

I named the author "<u>I AM</u>"

"The Author"

Written in my heart, Friday, April 6th, 2018

I have written you My heart's thoughts in My Word (Bible) to help my children learn from worldly history of all My people.

My words contain truth of examples and warnings to guard your heart against worse inclinations and lead your lives into wiser living.

Valuable lessons are learned from examining the lives of My children who have come before you.

From his heart into my Spirit: **I AM**

Dedication Letter to One I Miss!

To my wife, Doris, who left me on December 6th, 2016
to be with The Lord
Married thirty-six years

Honey I love you and always will. May God in His heavenly ways give you peace, joy and pleasure.

You battled heart disease from early childhood until God decided to take you home for Himself.

You were my inspiration to keep going no matter how life treated me and how many times I fail for trying.

This book, I know, would have made you happy because you always saw in me what God has seen in my character of Himself.

Thank you, Honey!

Love always,
Joe

Personal Letter to Each Brother and Sister in Christ

How to receive the most out of what you are about to read.

"<u>Pray First</u>" Pray to our Father to receive wisdom from His messages to be revealed in your heart.

"<u>Meditate Second</u>" Every message of each day will have a different understanding of what the Lord is sharing with you.

"<u>Thankfulness Third</u>" Thank our Lord and Savior Jesus Christ for what the Father has revealed to you and ask Him to place it permanently in your heart.

"<u>Final Thoughts</u>" The bottom of each page will offer four open spaces for personal thoughts of each message revealed.

May the Lord find Himself in your spirit forever.

Your Brother in CHRIST

January

JANUARY

1ST

1. To make a friend, **be a friend**. A genuine friend is a gift of My mercy and love.

2. Remember a **self-centered person** is not a Godly-centered person.

3. You are **never alone**, so do not try to live life apart from Me.

4. My child, when you **first came to Me**, it was an event, but becoming like Me will be a lifelong journey.

―――◆―――

Memo Notes

1.

2.

3.

4.

JANUARY

2ND

1. If any of My children see a brother or sister in need but has **no pity upon them**, how can thy blessings be upon them.

2. **The last word**, practice not to offer it.

3. I am the only thing **that is cause** for all things to work for good.

4. **Every new day** has been given to you by Me.

MEMO NOTES

1.

2.

3.

4.

JANUARY

3rd

1. **To find Me you** must be willing to seek Me in everything.

2. My child, **non-believers** of My Word are hesitant to trust Me because they do not know Me.

3. **It grieves Me** when any one of My children become jealous of another believer.

4. **The beauty of your outside** will surely disappear, but the beauty from your heart will continue forever.

Memo Notes

1.

2.

3.

4.

JANUARY

4ᵀᴴ

1. **The more you get to know Me**, the sooner you will find yourself in me.

2. Children, **stop Looking** at tomorrow without enjoying what you have received this day.

3. I know all your hurts, your worries, and fears. Why not speak to Me about them. **Am I** not your comforter, provider, and protector who listens?

4. Your **moments of weakness** have a pattern. Come to Me to change your course of action.

MEMO NOTES

1.

2.

3.

4.

JANUARY

5ᵀᴴ

1. **Good credit** is not needed to make it into My Kingdom. Only your faith in My Son Jesus Christ as Lord and Savior.

2. Your friends are an **extension of My love** toward you.

3. An **unforgiven spirit** will only poison your life.

4. When you learn to trust me **what if** will not enter your thoughts.

MEMO NOTES

1.

2.

3.

4.

JANUARY

6ᵗʰ

1. Every day that is **passing by** is one less day before My final return.

2. My days are also your days. **Let us enjoy** them together.

3. Do you know the **blood I bled** at Calvary is the same I have given to each of my children?

4. I will keep you day and night, **guarding your heart** and soul from danger

This is who I am.

Memo Notes

1.

2.

3.

4.

7ᵗʰ

1. Do not try to live outside of My will and My timing. You will be much **disappointed**.

2. I look at **every man's heart**. Man looks at man's appearance.

3. Exercise your faith in Me by **giving yourself** to others unconditionally.

4. Be **anxious for nothing**. It will only bring more anxiety into your life.

Memo Notes

1.

2.

3.

4.

JANUARY

8ᵀᴴ

1. You must **prepare your heart** before I can feed it the seeds of Heaven and plant into your life.

2. Be joyful, **always, have contentment** with what you have already received.

3. When you show mercy, you are **sharing with others** what I have already given into you.

4. I say to you, **trying times** are never a time to stop trying for what is righteous.

Memo Notes

1.

2.

3.

4.

JANUARY

9TH

1. To all My children, the only **protection** in your life that is needed is a relationship with my Son, "Jesus Christ".

2. Stay true to Me for **your rewards**. Heaven depends upon your obedience.

3. Always **give of self** at every moment of your life without reservation.

4. Ask your heart this question, **who are the happiest and most joyful** of my children? One whom accumulates wealth or shares what they have received with others.

Memo Notes

1.

2.

3.

4.

JANUARY

10ᵀᴴ

1. **Read My Word.** Meditate on it and My armor of protection will be upon you forever.

2. Your heart will **never become empty** or ever need filling as long as you come to Me as your supplier.

3. Do this for me. **Give your heart** to others. Many are seeking Me.

4. All who are **hungry for the Father's** love must come to Me first. I am the truth and the light to the Father's gateway of Heaven's fulfillments.

MEMO NOTES

1.

2.

3.

4.

JANUARY

11TH

1. The more you read about Me, **listen to Me** and **talk to Me**. Your burdens will have lost their desire.

2. Give **thanks to the Father** who has shared all His children with you.

3. When you **pray for others**, I will ask the Father to show mercy to all you have prayed for.

4. Keep Me always as your **front runner** in your thoughts. It will lead to harmony in your walk.

Memo Notes

1.

2.

3.

4.

JANUARY

12TH

1. Man is like the Dead Sea. **He receives much** of My living waters but gives back little to his brothers and sisters.

2. I am **only** a thought away!

3. To those who **disappoint you**, be a **friend**, not a buddy.

4. The closer you are to Me, the more time you are expected to spend with Me. **The world will become a stranger** to your heart and vanish into its sea.

Memo Notes

1.

2.

3.

4.

JANUARY

13TH

1. Nature is often **My nurse** for tired souls and weary bodies. Let her have her ways with you.

2. You will **never know** true peace in your heart until you give your heart away to Me.

3. Remember, **without Me** your life is completely on its own.

4. Many of my children consider me further from the truth, **how about you?**

MEMO NOTES

1.

2.

3.

4.

JANUARY

14TH

1. Wait on My timing for **hopeful expectation**. You will experience peace and joy that surpasses all understanding.

2. You are not to hate those brothers and sisters who **oppress you**. Ask Me alone for forgiveness of their action**s**.

3. When I permit trials in your life, I provide the **Father's comfort** from his spirit.

4. **Wisdom** is the capacity to see life through the Father's eyes.

MEMO NOTES

1.

2.

3.

4.

JANUARY

15TH

1. Focus on My power and ability to control **all circumstances**. The longer your thoughts on Me the smaller your problems will appear in your presence.

2. Only My ways, **not your ways** will protect your pathway.

3. Children, you wonder **where Heaven is**. Heaven is where I am. A place My heart has prepared for you.

4. Let each child know the **beauty of my world** is hidden within them.

Memo Notes

1.

2.

3.

4.

JANUARY

16th

1. I say to you living in faith of the unseen is the beginning of life; of your **kingdom to come** in My New Heaven.

2. What I allowed **on the cross** was a gift for all my children to have hope of eternal life.

3. **Following** Me demands your all!

4. All hardship is not bad. Much of it brings My children **closer to me** and the Father's way.

Memo Notes

1.

2.

3.

4.

JANUARY

17TH

1. Many of my children **obey Me more** when they have little to nothing to offer.

2. It is not how much you read about Me that matters, it is how much you get **to know who I am** through My Words.

3. The beauty of **My creation** lies within you.

4. My word will not only lead you day by day and year by year, but **step by step** will unfold your pathway of who I am.

Memo Notes

1.

2.

3.

4.

JANUARY

18ᵀᴴ

1. Open and allow Me to reach into your heart and **have me planted** to live there forever.

2. Prayer is your **direct line** of communication to the Father and **me**.

3. I am the **burden bearer**, pray unto Me of all your worries. Come to Me you who are heavy-laden and I will give you rest. Always share someone else's burdens. My grace is sufficient for all.

4. There are no moments that pass by that I do not **love you**.

Memo Notes

1.

2.

3.

4.

JANUARY

19th

1. Grow in the need to **share Me** with all others.

2. The Father sent Me to rule and reign over all mankind. **My sheep know my voice.** I abide in My Father's will and He is much pleased.

3. I will never live in a **dirty body**.

4. Much is placed upon my children's plate who are **Willing to Receive** what has been offered.

Memo Notes

1.

2.

3.

4.

20ᵀᴴ

1. Let no **thoughts of unkindness** dwell in your heart.

2. The ways of the world will change daily, but My **Love for the world** will never change.

3. When I give you **an assignment,** it comes with My enablement to see it through unto completion.

4. When you pray to Me, there are no waiting lines. My **Heart is always open** to hear my children's cry.

Memo Notes

1.

2.

3.

4.

JANUARY

21ˢᵗ

1. Burdens will become a **thing of the past** when you focus your eyes upon me.

2. **He is rich**, who is satisfied with what He has already received.

3. Child, **write My name** on your lips so that I may call on you by who is in you.

4. Live so that when someone gets to **know you**, they will want to also know the Father.

Memo Notes

1.

2.

3.

4.

JANUARY

22ND

1. Not all will **know My love** unless someone shows them first.

2. **Communication with Me** is not a want, it is always a need.

3. In bustle, so little is accomplished. **Take the calm** in me with you in the most hurried days.

4. The more you feast **on my words**, the healthier you will become.

Memo Notes

1.

2.

3.

4.

JANUARY

23ʳᵈ

1. Be **motivated by love**. All the Father and I know is love. It is a gift that all My children have received when first conceived.

2. Follow My Lamb everywhere **He leads** you. His direction is always made perfect.

3. Those with a pure heart will **desire My ways** more than their wants.

4. Your **heart is restless** until you find rest in Me. Come to me for my peace.

Memo Notes

1.

2.

3.

4.

JANUARY

24ᵀᴴ

1. **My fence** keeps you within My boundary of blessings. Why are you looking elsewhere?

2. Man cannot stand not being in charge of his own life. **Look where man** has taken him.

3. Give others My attention by **giving yourself** to them. Humble yourself before them and honor my father.

4. There is always time to pray for others. **Why not** make it a daily habit and start this day.

Memo Notes

1.

2.

3.

4.

25ᵀᴴ

1. Having I **created all things** for good and your pleasure, use what you have received wisely to honor the Father.

2. Once turned on, **the light** in your heart will shine bright to everyone who believes.

3. You will **never be sure** if tomorrow will come. Plan this day with Me.

4. Do I dwell **in your heart?** Let it be shown with each other.

Memo Notes

1.

2.

3.

4.

26TH

1. If your prayers and thoughts line up with the **Father's will**, I will honor them and seek the Father to fulfill them.

2. Engage in **all prayers** to the Father with praise and thanksgiving.

3. The **breath of continuous life** is upon My children when your life is given to My Son as your savior.

4. Your needs will **never exhaust** My supplies.

Memo Notes

1.

2.

3.

4.

27ᵀᴴ

1. Let me **plant into your heart** many seeds that need to grow. Water each seed with your prayers and My Words daily.

2. If **My wealth from inside** your heart is being wasted, how poor my children will become.

3. No one is lost **in the desert** who follows Me.

4. Prayers and **helplessness** are inseparable.

Memo Notes

1.

2.

3.

4.

28TH

1. My word offers a **Lifetime of GUARANTEES** if one follows my instruction book.

2. I am **your life** and the number of how many days.

3. Your faith in Me will grow best in the **winter of trials**. Be patient to endure what you receive. Spring is around the corner.

4. Child, **your belief** in Me is the substance of our relationship.

Memo Notes

1.

2.

3.

4.

JANUARY

29th

1. Everyone you **meet in life**, think of them as meeting Me.

2. Follow me through **life of** the **wilderness**. Never will I allow you to become lost or left alone.

3. The Bible is **my love letter** to you. Share this romance with others.

4. May my grace be seen upon you even when your kindness goes **unappreciated** in others.

Memo Notes

1.

2.

3.

4.

JANUARY

30TH

1. Real men are **My servants** to others. Serve without looking for man's approval.

2. Never forget that you are not what you do. You are who you are, **a child of Mine**.

3. Be like My Son, **a heart full of love** that wants to please others without reservations.

4. **Inadequacies** are a blessing to be thankful for. Each one is recognized by the Father who **loves** you **just** the way you are.

Memo Notes

1.

2.

3.

4.

JANUARY

31ST

1. Every time you **face a trial,** come to me to reshape your thoughts.

2. **Love your neighbor** as they are not how you wish them to please you.

3. Do not let your discouragement block your eyesight of my **awesome love** and power in you. Let it pass by.

4. Your life may be the **only Bible** someone else will read.

MEMO NOTES

1.

2.

3.

4.

February

FEBRUARY

1ST

1. **Give me your heart** so I may mend each piece of brokenness, one part at a time.

2. Your prayers are as **important to me** as your breathing is to you.

3. Man's heart makes up what he believes is truth. **I am the only truth** worth trusting.

4. Tough times are only **for a season** to those who place their trust in Me.

Memo Notes

1.

2.

3.

4.

FEBRUARY

2ND

1. When praying to the Father, let your words **flow naturally** from your heart.

2. My church **is a hospital** for all to be healed and made whole.

3. Through **each hardship** you endure, I will make Myself known.

4. Expect great things from Me. Attempt great things to **please the Father.**

MEMO NOTES

1.

2.

3.

4.

FEBRUARY

3ʳᵈ

1. Keep nothing to yourself that the Father reveals to you. **Open your heart** to share it with many.

2. After every good Friday, there will **always be an Easter** to those who live for Me.

3. Living your **faith in Me** is believing I will honor My Word no matter what has taken place.

4. **Give your time**, stillness, and patience to listen to Me.

Memo Notes

1.

2.

3.

4.

FEBRUARY

4TH

1. When digested, My Word will nourish your mind, your emotions and **fulfill my will.**

2. Only **worship your giver**, none of your gifts.

3. I do not delay My second and final coming. **My children delay** my mercy from expiring.

4. Never forget you have a **higher calling** to achieve as a servant of the Most High.

Memo Notes

1.

2.

3.

4.

FEBRUARY

5ᵗʰ

1. The world has only one purpose; to keep my **peace and joy** from entering your heart and others.

2. I and **The Father** are one, never divided as two.

3. My love is like a **pipeline.** It flows like a river of water through your life. Keep your faucet open to receive even more.

4. Do not become **overcome by worldly evil,** but overcome evil with good.

Memo Notes

1.

2.

3.

4.

FEBRUARY

6ᵗʰ

1. My sons and daughters, if you look through My eyes, **you will see** a world in need of a savior.

2. Many sins of man are **acting independently** of the father's will. That can cause him pain.

3. When you fall to the ground, I am here to pick up **your broken pieces** and reconstruct them until they become one.

4. If it is **unclean,** let it go!

Memo Notes

1.

2.

3.

4.

FEBRUARY

7TH

1. My death on the cross brings life. My death and resurrection **will save many.**

2. Sometimes I allow **great trials** so you can learn greater faith.

3. You are **loved by the Father** beyond imagination!

4. My Word is a **product of the Father's will**. It reveals how he wants his children to live.

Memo Notes

1.

2.

3.

4.

8ᵗʰ

1. The most balance **Christ-like children** I have, are those who read My Word with an open heart.

2. My child, the larger your **thoughts about me**, the smaller your thoughts about your problems will become.

3. Prayer **does not change the Father**. It only changes my children's lives.

4. Even when you are **unfaithful** to My Word, I am always faithful to you.

―――◆―――

Memo Notes

1.

2.

3.

4.

FEBRUARY

9ᵀᴴ

1. What matters to most of my children is shown on **the outside**. What matters to the Father comes from within their hearts.

2. To know of Me, is not the same as **knowing me**. Meditate on My Word!

3. Your time is **in my hands**. Recognize how important you are to Me.

4. **Be patient with others** as I have been with you.

Memo Notes

1.

2.

3.

4.

FEBRUARY

10ᵀᴴ

1. My promise to you with certainty, is always **keeping My word**.

2. I am a **sovereign God**, always delivering unexpected plans in each of My children's lives.

3. How are you **living out your life**; for yourself or the glory of his name?

4. Spiritual **health care** is written in My Words.

Memo Notes

1.

2.

3.

4.

FEBRUARY

11TH

1. Plant into your heart My word and **watch it grow** into a beautiful garden of everlasting love.

2. My child, **apart from Me**, you will not function in the Father's wisdom.

3. **Share with one another.** Nobody cares how much you know until they know how much you care for others.

4. You must **stay focused** in my word to understand what has been said.

Memo Notes

1.

2.

3.

4.

FEBRUARY

12TH

1. **Brotherly kindness.** Be trustworthy among each brother and sister. Share all your blessings including thyself.

2. The foundation of my Church has been built upon my Son Jesus Christ, the **Cornerstone** of all its Temple.

3. One must be a **giver of thyself** if you are going to be a follower of Mine.

4. Wherever your path leads you, **be assured** I am also sharing the journey.

Memo Notes

1.

2.

3.

4.

FEBRUARY

13ᵗʰ

1. Enjoy each day with Me. I will bring **peace and happiness** in your lives.

2. **World without sin.** Heaven awaits those that Believe in me as LORD and SAVIOR.

3. Give **gentleness** in all your thoughts toward others.

4. **Remember** I am always working in your life to accomplish My divine purpose within you.

Memo Notes

1.

2.

3.

4.

FEBRUARY

14TH

1. My delivery of **promises to all My children** are never too late. They were pre-arranged before they were created.

2. Many people will become your buddy, but only a few will be called friend.

3. I have promised to impact you with the **Father's wisdom** if you only ask.

4. In My **store house** are many blessings awaiting you; live a righteous life to receive them.

MEMO NOTES

1.

2.

3.

4.

FEBRUARY

15TH

1. No man is that **wicked** who cannot be saved.

2. Joy is **my reward** as if it were your heart's response to My smile of recognition of your faithfulness.

3. Give thanks **for the children** you have received for My kingdom is full of each one's beauty.

4. Wisdom and **perfected action** come through seeking Me and following my Father's will.

MEMO NOTES

1.

2.

3.

4.

FEBRUARY

16TH

1. Godliness enjoyed with **contentment** is all the Father has asked.

2. People **need the Lord**. I beg of you to receive of what has been offered.

3. Believers of Mine know how to **give back to others** of themselves.

4. The **secret to peace** is sharing and placing your worries and cares upon my hands.

MEMO NOTES

1.

2.

3.

4.

FEBRUARY

17TH

1. My children who unconditionally give of themselves without expecting a return are My **caregivers**.

2. **More of Me** is always available for the asking.

3. The busier your day, the more time you should **spend in prayer** preparing.

4. **Mission field:** You are my church. Be my worldwide rescue mission of man's destination.

MEMO NOTES

1.

2.

3.

4.

FEBRUARY

18TH

1. **Men of little faith.** Long prayers are shared in my Temple, short prayers are said in a storm.

2. **Live out My gospel** and watch others pursue your faith.

3. My message to you in a storm is to **slow life down and wait** till it passes on.

4. So **many trials** become so many benefits when your life depends on Me.

MEMO NOTES

1.

2.

3.

4.

FEBRUARY

19TH

1. As much as I love you, I **always reject sin** in man's life.

2. I am **uninfluenced by circumstances**. My promise is kept. I am here, one with you in tender loving friendship to share your life unconditionally.

3. The glory of living is **to love and to be loved**, to give and to receive, and to serve and be served. Everyone caring for each other becomes a marriage that is inseparable.

4. I use many **unworthy children** to become My holy disciples.

MEMO NOTES

1.

2.

3.

4.

FEBRUARY

20TH

1. To choke your life with **worldly worries** will cause your heart to work harder. Lean on Me for a worry-free spirit!

2. Heed to My voice. It speaks slowly and clearly to those **hearts that will listen**.

3. **Smiles do not cost** anything except happiness given to others.

4. Whenever you are in danger, **My presence** will be near. Call for me in prayer.

Memo Notes

1.

2.

3.

4.

FEBRUARY

21ˢᵀ

1. **Be slow to anger!** Be patient always with your brothers and sisters.

2. The well of My **living water** is within you. Drink from it to be satisfied.

3. **Can anyone** affirm My Word untrue?

4. Patiently **I was** there all the time
   Patiently **I am** there all the time
   Patiently **I will** be there all the time
   What are my children waiting for?

Memo Notes

1.

2.

3.

4.

FEBRUARY

22ND

1. Lighten your load My child. **Live your life** with your weight placed on my shoulders.

2. **"My cross."** Love my son because he first loved you.

3. Control your thinking. Do not focus on your circumstances. **Cry out** to me in need.

4. Losing My salt in your life is **catastrophic** to my children.

Memo Notes

1.

2.

3.

4.

FEBRUARY

23ᴿᴰ

1. Let your heart dwell in serving each other. **Your reward** awaits you in Heaven.

2. Do not worry about **things that have not happened**. Where do those thoughts take you?

3. **Steward your time.** Too much on your plate will spoil quickly.

4. Disengage in **stress. Read my word** daily.

Memo Notes

1.

2.

3.

4.

FEBRUARY

24TH

1. Refuse what is not yours. **Allow nothing to be kept** in your heart that has not been conformed from the Father's will.

2. **No other way can one** be saved than through my son, Jesus Christ.

3. **Spiritual stability:** God of peace will always be with you.

4. **Educational failure** is not available of My word.

MEMO NOTES

1.

2.

3.

4.

FEBRUARY

25TH

1. When you think about Me for what you have received, you are also **thanking the Father** who had allowed it to be shared.

2. If you are a **stranger to prayer,** then you are also a stranger to my power.

3. Be a good steward of your works. The **Father will honor** your obedience with his reward.

4. At times I will turn up the heat of your trials to **cleanse and purify** your heart to sanctify your soul.

Memo Notes

1.

2.

3.

4.

FEBRUARY

26ᵀᴴ

1. Only seek **material things** when that effort will cause an increase for the Father's Kingdom.

2. The one who places Me first in their heart is headed for **eternal happiness**.

3. Seek the things from above, **selfishness** will soon disappear.

4. Praying daily will **never close doors,** only open much more.

MEMO NOTES

1.

2.

3.

4.

FEBRUARY

27TH

1. Love is mercy **full of God.**

2. Self-focus and self-centered is naturally selfish. **Be others' center.**

3. Improve your attitude to have **pure gratitude.** Your heart will enjoy it mostly.

4. Jealousy is a product of your flesh. Shake it out until it **empties itself** from your heart.

Memo Notes

1.

2.

3.

4.

FEBRUARY

28ᵀᴴ

1. If My message **leads you**, share it with others.

2. Failure in your life is going to happen. I seek it as **work in progress**. Learn from its works.

3. **Spiritual laziness** is a landmine!

4. Take My hand, hold it tight, and **never let go**. Your life will never be left alone.

Memo Notes

1.

2.

3.

4.

FEBRUARY

29TH

1. **Allow the love of Me** within you to spill over to the ones you love and cherish.

2. **Communicate with Me**. My lines are always open.

3. Be accountable for **all your actions**. It will make your life much wiser.

4. How much time would the **world need changing** if everyone spent more time on their knees.

———◆———

MEMO NOTES

1.

2.

3.

4.

March

MARCH

1ST

1. **Mothers and Fathers**, how can you ask your children to abide in My Word while your life is living outside of the Father's will?

2. When I **chastise you with My discipline** it is good for your soul. It will bring needed dependency on Me.

3. **Forgiveness** must be granted as many times as it is asked.

4. Do you believe in miracles? **You are one.**

MEMO NOTES

1.

2.

3.

4.

MARCH

2ᴺᴰ

1. **Cries of your heart**, I see them weeping for my comfort.

2. How did you feel when you **walked out of the wilderness** and found Me awaiting on the other side?

3. You may have **everything on this Earth,** but do you have all of Me in your heart.

4. How are your **daily prayers** and obeying my word register on a scale of one through ten? Less than ten, you are not listening!

Memo Notes

1.

2.

3.

4.

MARCH

3rd

1. I am **your Lord**, **your Father** and **best friend.** What a partnership we share with one another.

2. Do your brothers and sisters smell the **life fragrance** of Jesus in you?

3. It takes me to raise your children holy. Learn to **depend on My teachings.**

4. A **Christian life** should be lived daily, not weekly.

Memo Notes

1.

2.

3.

4.

MARCH

4ᵀᴴ

1. I will ask the Father for another advocate placed upon you. **The Holy Spirit of his Truth.**

2. Recharge your life on the Sabbath. Keep it holy. **A day of refreshment and rest.**

3. **My Children's Care:** depend upon Me.

4. A cause for rejoicing. I came to **save man's life.**

Memo Notes

1.

2.

3.

4.

MARCH

5th

1. Taking me on will be a **lifetime burden**, but no other burdens will be so satisfying.

2. Your **labors in life** should always be headed by My pathway.

3. You are not to love under the law, but under **My grace**.

4. **Man's final Heartbeat:** When you get to the finished line of your life, where will that have taken you?

Memo Notes

1.

2.

3.

4.

6ᵗʰ

1. All I ask is a relationship with you. I am a very **jealous God**.

2. Is your ship **carried by My Word** or is it cruising alone in the wind?

3. Second to loving me is **loving thoughts around you,** and not the worldly things you possess.

4. **Do not be tied** to the foolishness of this world, it leads to false hope.

Memo Notes

1.

2.

3.

4.

MARCH

7TH

1. **Kindness and gentleness** are the makeup we wear in Heaven. Why not give samples out to one another?

2. **Live with Me children.** Know always where you rest.

3. I am the **flower of purity.** Absorb and be refreshed with my fragrance.

4. Never give something to others that **has not been given to you** first from above.

Memo Notes

1.

2.

3.

4.

MARCH

8TH

1. You have been made perfect until you live life outside My will. **Realign your life** where most needed.

2. Let out all within you that has been hidden from Me. **Let it go forever!**

3. Lift your eyes toward Heaven to see the glory of My Kingdom. **Share your sight** with each of My children.

4. Thinking the thoughts of Me is always **Biblical thinking**.

Memo Notes

1.

2.

3.

4.

MARCH

9TH

1. My thoughts are **not of yours.** Only my children are asked to follow them through.

2. Do not allow **sinful deception** to enter your heart. Hold firmly to My Word.

3. Enter My rest. **Encourage each other** into the body of Christ.

4. Kingship of Christ **belongs to Me**.

Memo Notes

1.

2.

3.

4.

MARCH

10TH

1. A **believing Christian** who follows Me has a new identity in this world.

2. Beware, truth is **more important than facts**. The facts My children may receive in the world may conflict with what My truth has spoken.

3. Nothing will change in your life until you **change your heart** in me.

4. A saved Christian **will not lust** after the flesh outside of their marriage.

Memo Notes

1.

2.

3.

4.

MARCH

11th

1. I have given you GOD'S children to **expand his Kingdom.** Raise them wisely.

2. **Feed My sheep.** Give them what they need, and I will give them what they want.

3. **Carelessness** can become stupidity. Be careful how you reveal My Word to others.

4. Are there any words in My book that are not speaking **the father's truth?**

Memo Notes

1.

2.

3.

4.

MARCH

12ᵀᴴ

1. Nothing in your life will ever **be shut** from my eyes.

2. Taking handouts is hard labor. Come to Me for **rest and plenty**. My storehouse is full and satisfying for the asking.

3. My son **cleanses your body** like no one else can.

4. Do not **breed sin**, it will always overtake your life.

Memo Notes

1.

2.

3.

4.

MARCH

13ᵗʰ

1. As a believer in Christ, **what excuse** may I explain to the Father of my children who do not share His word on the Sabbath that He would understand?

2. **Living for the moment.** How long will that last?

3. Draw to Me first and **I will submit** my life into yours forever.

4. You will **always stumble in life** when you disobey My Words.

Memo Notes

1.

2.

3.

4.

MARCH

14TH

1. **Get connected.** My children of believers are a holy nation among each other. A total body in Christ!

2. When your **hands are raised** toward Heaven and your tears come down, I will dry up all your sorrows with my flesh.

3. Recognize My love in those who **convict you.** Search for it until it has been found.

4. **What comes around**, goes around. Let us share one another in My holy circle.

Memo Notes

1.

2.

3.

4.

MARCH

15ᵗʰ

1. Living a life **without me**. How disappointing you have become towards your Father's will.

2. **Let Me shape you!** I will build My house upon you and through you, until it becomes complete by My cornerstone.

3. Your **new birth** in Me. Where will it lead you? To your new home in my kingdom.

4. I may **chasten you** for many a season until I am able to use you for My glory.

Memo Notes

1.

2.

3.

4.

MARCH

16ᵗʰ

1. If you have tasted my **graciousness**, consume it within your spirit and walk with it everywhere it leads you.

2. Turn to **my cross** and the devil will flee from thy path.

3. Do you **know with certainty** what tomorrow brings and who you will be sharing it with?

4. Bring all **your desires** to me and I will extinguish those that are none of Mine.

Memo Notes

1.

2.

3.

4.

MARCH

17TH

1. When your brothers or sisters cause **sin against you**, they are also committing this sin against my father.

2. Why are you **afraid of failing** and disappointing your friends? Are they really a friend or just a buddy needing something out of your life?

3. I have **no patterns** for My children who need to be healed. Each child's hurts are submitted to the Father's will as one.

4. The only **Door of heaven** that will be open are through my pathway.

Memo Notes

1.

2.

3.

4.

MARCH

18ᵀᴴ

1. **Human Goodness** will never take my children to Heaven, only their belief in my son JESUS CHRIST as Lord and Savior.

2. To know **My truth**, nothing but My truth, read My Word daily.

3. Letting go of Me will cause your world to crumble. **Come back to me.** Let us start a new life together.

4. Is every word flowing out of your mouth **purified water** or a curse full of man's lies?

MEMO NOTES

1.

2.

3.

4.

MARCH

19ᵗʰ

1. Be only **impatient** for My directions but be patient to wait on them.

2. Forgive them who **hurt you**. Do not stone them anymore.

3. Failure **teaches believers** that it is much wiser and more profitable to be obedient to the Lord.

4. Be anxious for nothing. My **timing is made perfect**. Waiting is a lesson of trust.

Memo Notes

1.

2.

3.

4.

MARCH

20th

1. **Why pray** when you can always worry. Worry takes life nowhere, but prayer keeps in touch with the one who handles all concerns.

2. All and everything I can do in your life will last with **eternal value**.

3. Be **strong and courageous**. Courage comes when your faith in Me is stronger than your fears in life.

4. **Trust Me more** than you trust yourself and see what will become of your faith.

Memo Notes

1.

2.

3.

4.

MARCH

21ᔆᵀ

1. You are being molded into **My image** through trials.

2. My Spirit is **like the wind.** You know I am there but never seen.

3. **The GREAT sin!** Man is a sinner when his own heart defies the belief of who I am.

4. Service is not something **you do for me**, but something I do through you for others.

Memo Notes

1.

2.

3.

4.

MARCH

22ND

1. Prayer is **your bridge** between my peace and emotional stress.

2. When My trials have **achieved their goal** in your life, I will remove them one at a time.

3. Being persistent is **about doing**, even as you wait patiently for results.

4. Understanding will tell you **what is happening**. My wisdom will tell you why!

Memo Notes

1.

2.

3.

4.

MARCH

23ᴿᴰ

1. Let your **foundation of faith** be established by My promise.

2. Your faith is **tested**, so that you may trust My faithfulness.

3. All you **can imagine** that is good for man is from the Father's will.

4. If I am **honored in your heart**, I will also be honored in the Father's spirit.

Memo Notes

1.

2.

3.

4.

MARCH

24ᵀᴴ

1. **Let My Word** fill your memory and rule over your heart with guidance.

2. True success is measured by the Father in your **obedience toward me**.

3. How can you comfort me? **Care and Love each other.**

4. **Making fun** of others is always a bad example of my love.

Memo Notes

1.

2.

3.

4.

MARCH

25TH

1. Share Me in **your daily walk** with your brothers and sisters in Christ. Allow My presence to be known.

2. **HOSPITALITY.** Am I Always welcomed in your life?

3. There is no cover charge to enter My gates. The only requirement is to **give your life** to my son, Jesus Christ.

4. I will have prepared all your **needs in heaven** before you shall receive them.

Memo Notes

1.

2.

3.

4.

MARCH

26TH

1. Come to me with your **Heart of stone** and I will cleanse it of its unforgiveness.

2. **Filling your heart** with Me. How nutritious that will become.

3. Place My name first upon your daily schedule. Let us see how much we can **accomplish together** in prayer.

4. Keep praying and asking to **receive my thoughts** into your heart. My answer may be shared in others.

MEMO NOTES

1.

2.

3.

4.

27TH

1. Keep **your heart pure** so I will not need to judge you.

2. Your body was designed **for your pleasure** and My righteousness. Keep it clean and pure to honor his name.

3. **My sweet lamb**, whom I love dearly, gave His life freely so that my children may live forever.

4. Children, **clean up My world** and make it whole again.

Memo Notes

1.

2.

3.

4.

MARCH

28ᵀᴴ

1. Do not fear **My discipline**. It corrects impurities in the Heart.

2. Your **weeping for others** is part of my strength that is needed when others are hurting.

3. How sad is it for God's children who **reject My word.**

4. Be **not connected** to this world for where you live has become dirty.

Memo Notes

1.

2.

3.

4.

MARCH

29ᵀᴴ

1. **No one else** but The Father's gate will be kept open when rejected by man.

2. See only what I see in man's life. **Nothing else matters.**

3. Open your heart each morning with praise. **Receive His thoughts.** Allow the spirit of The Father to cultivate your mind.

4. Share with others how **perishable life** will become without Me.

Memo Notes

1.

2.

3.

4.

MARCH

30ᵗʰ

1. My love **endures forever.** No one is loved more or any less. I love each child the same. They are mine to love forever.

2. Fulfill your heart with the **Father's thoughts.** Allow each to be absorbed in your spirit.

3. I will apply wisdom to man's heart who **Seeks My truth.**

4. Do not worship the ground you walk. Only one is worthy of praise, **I AM.**

MEMO NOTES

1.

2.

3.

4.

MARCH

31ST

1. Be **anxious for nothing** but be content for all that travels on your pathway.

2. **Every step** you walk, expect not to be alone.

3. You cannot **Walk with me** each day without your life being changed.

4. **Love your enemies** as much as your friends. Sometimes, love them even more.

MEMO NOTES

1.

2.

3.

4.

April

APRIL

1ST

1. Always remember who your life is **representing.**

2. Allow yourself to receive as much as you **share with others.** My kingdom is full of all who share.

3. Church, why do My children share My temple as one? **Worship my Father!**

4. It is not how long you worship the Father, but **how much time you listen** for His voice.

Memo Notes

1.

2.

3.

4.

APRIL

2ND

1. How much **time is wasted** of your life by arguing with a brother?

2. Bringing your brothers and sisters to My Son for their salvation can become **quite a journey**. Do no give up when they refuse. Rest a while and try again.

3. Let my children **seek in your life** what their Hearts have been searching for.

4. All that **I am** was **made perfect**! Yesterday, today, and forevermore.

MEMO NOTES

1.

2.

3.

4.

APRIL

3ʳᵈ

1. Let the **Bread of Life** that is given to you be enough. Always pray with Thanksgiving of everything I have placed into your heart.

2. You **hear My spoken words clearly** because you are listening from your heart.

3. Never live your life by feelings. Live it by **reading and acting upon My word**.

4. Everything you **see, hear, and touch** has always been a part of Me.

Memo Notes

1.

2.

3.

4.

APRIL

4TH

1. **You are worthy** to be placed on top of My schedule.

2. Each day I am adding more and more to your heart's **contentment**.

3. Whether you speak clearly or **mumble your words**, I always hear clearly from your heart.

4. **Manly flesh only wants** to hear what man desires, not what his life is looking for.

Memo Notes

1.

2.

3.

4.

APRIL

5TH

1. The Truth I share with you this day is **the only Truth** that is shared in my Heavenly kingdom.

2. It is not how much you **accomplish in life** that matters, but how much of life you live out for Me.

3. **Fear is formed in the world,** none of Me and none of you.

4. The desires in your heart to **have it now** will only last for a season minus a lifetime of satisfaction.

Memo Notes

1.

2.

3.

4.

APRIL

6TH

1. Love and **pray for everyone** in your heart who you love and whom you disagree with.

2. **It has been written.** I will share My love with you forever.

3. Increase **your love for Me** by sharing My love in you in others.

4. **No time schedules** in Heaven, only the right moments.

Memo Notes

1.

2.

3.

4.

APRIL

7TH

1. Live your life for **moments of Me**.

2. **Kindness costs so little.** How much love and sharing of kindness do you share with each other?

3. The best way to learn My ways is to **obey My word** in your heart always.

4. Why are many of my **children saddened**? Have they lost their purpose and faith to follow the Father's will? Begin again, come again. He is awaiting your return.

Memo Notes

1.

2.

3.

4.

APRIL

8TH

1. **Listener**: Prayer is a two-way street, both must give an ear to hear the other speaking.

2. Let Me lead you to My reservoir of **living waters**. Drink from it and be satisfied.

3. There is not one day **ahead of your path** that I have not seen before you enter.

4. Read My words with **compassion**. Many of My children live their lives upon its love.

Memo Notes

1.

2.

3.

4.

APRIL

9ᵀᴴ

1. The journey to **truthful living** is upon you. Enjoy each day as it is given to you by faith.

2. Place in your heart the **love of Me** toward others.

3. Never turn away a **child who is talking**. It could be I whose voice is speaking.

4. How many times do you forgive your brothers who sins? Until the **Kingdom of Heaven** has come upon you.

Memo Notes

1.

2.

3.

4.

APRIL

10TH

1. Seek my kingdom with only **love and contentment**.

2. When **self comes first**, peace will not follow.

3. If you desire a **successful marriage**, shed God's light upon it.

4. Nothing in this world will bring satisfaction to your soul. **Only a relationship with My son.**

MEMO NOTES

1.

2.

3.

4.

APRIL

11ᵀᴴ

1. **When I speak** into your spirit, you will know it is **I** doing the speaking.

2. Reach deep into your heart. What you have been **searching for** will be found.

3. All of what I have ever asked for is My **children sharing** with one another.

4. The power of the Father in me is in his **W--D**.

Memo Notes

1.

2.

3.

4.

APRIL

12ᵀᴴ

1. The **helper from above** is in His words carrying all your provisions through His Spirit.

2. No number is needed to call me, only a **cry from your Heart** will I answer.

3. Your heart is **listening more** because your spirit is asking more questions.

4. If material things become your God, then **I will never know YOU!**

Memo Notes

1.

2.

3.

4.

APRIL

13ᵀᴴ

1. I am your **teacher** and **his truth** follow me to know the father.

2. Let your sadness be brought to my throne so I may turn it away and **bring you much joy**.

3. Only one can share the difference in the world to My children. **My Father** through me.

4. I accomplished on the cross what the laws could not. **Forgiveness.**

Memo Notes

1.

2.

3.

4.

APRIL

14TH

1. **Life brilliancy** shines on Me through each of My children.

2. See life at its best. **See it through Me.**

3. Let me take your unhappiness and **redeem it** fully.

4. My child **do not be impatient** in an impatient world.

MEMO NOTES

1.

2.

3.

4.

APRIL

15ᵗʰ

1. No other way can I describe the Father's heart. **He is with you always.**

2. What you miss from not **hearing My voice,** I will plant in your heart forever.

3. Come to me for a **worry-free life.**

4. There is **nothing you can do** to stop My unconditional love from approaching you.

Memo Notes

1.

2.

3.

4.

APRIL

16ᵀᴴ

1. Give My love freely to others by showing them **you sincerely care**.

2. The **unseen to come** is mine. To believe in it is yours.

3. **Have a relationship** with one who will never criticize you. My Son!

4. When you live out and **keep my commandments**, you become the primary beneficiary.

Memo Notes

1.

2.

3.

4.

APRIL

17TH

1. Do you have what I have in Me? **If not, ask!**

2. **Always be thankful** from your heart, speak from your heart and act only through it.

3. Evil thoughts will divide your mind in **times of weakness.**

4. Count ALL MY JOY as a **spiritual blessing**.

MEMO NOTES

1.

2.

3.

4.

APRIL

18ᵀᴴ

1. **Never underestimate** the power of planting a seed.

2. Do not waste a **day of sorrows**. Grow from each one of them.

3. Those who seek Me as **the Bread of Life** will never go hungry.

4. If your heart is **full of Me**, expose it to others.

Memo Notes

1.

2.

3.

4.

APRIL

19th

1. **Heaven awaits** all My children. But are My children searching for Gods kingdom?

2. If you realize how much of you is **part of me**, let all of Me live within you.

3. To brighten another's day is a **merciful act** engaged toward Me.

4. The **Source of My Spirit** are the words of the Father.

Memo Notes

1.

2.

3.

4.

APRIL

20TH

1. What you receive in your spirit must be **devoured in your heart** and distributed upon others.

2. Many of My sheep may not recognize my voice. Speak **clearly from your heart** so they know it is I who is speaking.

3. **Open the door** to your heart and I will surely come in.

4. All **My sheep** have names. Everyone who hears my voice will come.

Memo Notes

1.

2.

3.

4.

APRIL

21ST

1. Live My **Father's will** to be satisfied.

2. **Pride in one's life** is natural. There are good and bad. Allow good pride to shine through you. Guard your heart against bad. It is unholy!

3. **Temptation to Sin** leads man's Heart to his grave when giving way to sin.

4. Start your day in prayer with my (**Cornerstone**) Jesus and he will build your day.

Memo Notes

1.

2.

3.

4.

APRIL

22ᴺᴰ

1. I ask My children **who know Me** to help others know me.

2. **Lord of all:** My father and your LORD is the same yesterday and remains the same tomorrow.

3. Give away child, what I have given to you freely. **My Love.**

4. **Bring others to Me** so they may also share my kingdom with you.

MEMO NOTES

1.

2.

3.

4.

APRIL

23ʳᵈ

1. What you fill your mind of Me, is **trustworthy**.

2. Keep the world from your heart and you will **hear Me** more clearly.

3. Always give from the heart what is **pure and innocent**.

4. By love, **serve each other** as a slave.

Memo Notes

1.

2.

3.

4.

APRIL

24ᴛʜ

1. It **pleases Me** when you are patiently waiting for My help.

2. Be thankful for everything, even in your **darkest days**.

3. Keep everything in your heart **pure and sacred**.

4. **Love your enemies** as you have loved your friends.

Memo Notes

1.

2.

3.

4.

APRIL

25ᵀᴴ

1. Reading My book will have **life's answers**.

2. I hear you, **but do you hear Me** when I am speaking?

3. Let your day begin with love and end **with joy**.

4. Be a **joyful giver** from your heart and not a taker of its joy.

Memo Notes

1.

2.

3.

4.

APRIL

26TH

1. **Discouragement** is man's choice.

2. Let your **hands open** to receive. Let your heart open to share.

3. Your time with each other is worth more than money. **Spend each moment wisely!**

4. Remember! **Eternal life** is the only one that will last forever.

Memo Notes

1.

2.

3.

4.

APRIL

27ᵀᴴ

1. Those in this world who know Me are but few. Their light shines **brighter in their hearts** than any stars in My Heaven.

2. **Take stress out** of your life and you will have much joy.

3. I love you unconditionally, even **when your ways fail Me**.

4. Fight the evil forces of this world **in My power** on your knees.

Memo Notes

1.

2.

3.

4.

APRIL

28ᵀᴴ

1. Rely on My wisdom to guide you. Rely on My truth to lead you. Rely on My love to **provide and protect**.

2. Let My children know **how much I love** them by sharing the life in you.

3. My child, you must live as I ask of you. **The Father's love** needs to be shared as written.

4. **Be a servant of all.** Take care of my bride.

Memo Notes

1.

2.

3.

4.

APRIL

29ᵀᴴ

1. All bridges cross to **The Father's house** through Me.

2. A heart that is open and **receives My voice** will always have a healthy spirit.

3. Let your heart **represent My Son** in everyone you seek.

4. Meditate on my son **day and night** to find yourself in him.

Memo Notes

1.

2.

3.

4.

30TH

1. Never say yes to a promise you make to the Father unless your **heart is fully in it**.

2. Come to **My open arms** to the gates of Heaven. Receive My Son as your Lord and Savior.

3. You are a holy child because **I am holy!**

4. Men who **speak from their hearts** will have much pleasures to share.

Memo Notes

1.

2.

3.

4.

May

1ˢᵗ

1. **Always pray** for others. **Always share** with others. **Always care** for others. Give all of self without expecting a return.

2. **Man's wisdom** will not solve man's problems.

3. Each week **take an inventory** of your life. See where you have been merciful and grateful to others.

4. Do you **care enough** to bear a brother's burden?

Memo Notes

1.

2.

3.

4.

MAY

2ⁿᵈ

1. I came to **redeem** the world. I will come again to **reign over** it.

2. **Within Me** there is a life that never ends.

3. Craving for anything in your heart other than Me will **bring much disappointment**.

4. Man tries to **nurture and possess material** things but rejects what he can share of my promises in his heart.

Memo Notes

1.

2.

3.

4.

MAY

3RD

1. My Heaven offers **endless time** without ever ending your life.

2. Let your enemies **never become enemies** of your heart.

3. Only **thoughts of Me** come from the heart.

4. You will **never be familiar** of My thoughts until you become uneasy reading My word.

MEMO NOTES

1.

2.

3.

4.

MAY

4ᵀᴴ

1. In you lies My **kingdom of Heaven**. Seek it and share it with all My sheep.

2. There is no **need for worries** once your life is full in Me.

3. As a flower grows with the sun and rain, let your heart **become like Me** as I feed and water it with the Father's cultivation.

4. The **peace of Me** quiets man's anxious heart.

Memo Notes

1.

2.

3.

4.

MAY

5ᵗʰ

1. **Never keep sadness** in your heart. Bring all your feelings to Me. I will share joy and peace to your unhappiness.

2. There is no debating with My words. **It has been written.**

3. What **words in My book** are outdated?

4. Continue to follow My **instruction book**. It will not lead your life into failure.

Memo Notes

1.

2.

3.

4.

6TH

1. Anything **outside My will** is foolishness.

2. Believe in Me with all your heart, all the time, and unbeliefs will **become vapors** in the air.

3. Allow much of Me in your heart and **allow much more** to be spoken through it.

4. I have **clothed you** with linens of My spirit.

Memo Notes

1.

2.

3.

4.

MAY

7ᵗʰ

1. You come to Me because you have believed in what My words say, **the Truth**.

2. **Be full of My light.** It is pure and sanctified.

3. It is the motive behind each of My children who know Me that **I cherish most**.

4. The more you focus on **living your life for me,** the more happiness I will deliver into your heart.

———◆———

Memo Notes

1.

2.

3.

4.

MAY

8ᵗʰ

1. My heart is an **open book** for all children to read.

2. Think before you speak, think before you act, and **think twice** before you walk away from me.

3. All roads do not lead to **Heaven,** only one. "**Born again** "

4. When your **lights go out**, rejoice for I am with you in darkness.

Memo Notes

1.

2.

3.

4.

9TH

1. Are my children aware of what they will first receive when they enter my gates?

    Washing away all their tears.

2. My **family of children** live in a world of unbelievers who do not understand your love for me.

3. **Make no mistake**, you cannot live forever without me.

4. Find **My joy** in all your struggles as it is there for the taking.

MEMO NOTES

1.

2.

3.

4.

MAY

10th

1. **Breathe in My spirit** and breathe out thyself.

2. Run My race with all **endurance**. My power and strength will assist your completion.

3. **Your keeper:** I am always there. No one asked me to be there except the father.

4. You can be a follower of my father, but do you **follow his ways?**

Memo Notes

1.

2.

3.

4.

MAY

11TH

1. You will never be placed on **call waiting** for the Father who hears your voice. He will answer before you dial.

2. Having your new life in Me changes your title in the world: **Trader!**

3. **Energize your life** with prayer.

4. Bring your **evil thoughts** of others to Me to cleanse them out of your heart.

MEMO NOTES

1.

2.

3.

4.

MAY

12ᵀᴴ

1. **Your citizenship** in the world is only temporary. Make and do your best for now. For My glory and your future rewards are awaiting.

2. The beauty of **serving the Father** surpasses all understanding with much joy.

3. Let your **heart speak** louder than words.

4. Always fill your heart and tongue with My **grateful thinking**. Do not allow your old self to speak once more.

Memo Notes

1.

2.

3.

4.

13ᵗʰ

1. Receive Me in your heart to **wash you in My love** and have My Son rinse away your sins.

2. Be so **joyful** to the ones you love.

3. I am your Father and you are My **glory forever**.

4. **When you speak** without love, it is only a noise I receive.

Memo Notes

1.

2.

3.

4.

MAY

14TH

1. Be generous always. **How generous** have I been with you?

2. Listen before you speak so My voice may be **heard clearly**.

3. Never turn your heart the other way from a child who **ignores you**. Be compassionate and merciful always.

4. My love is an **open book** to those who want to receive it.

MEMO NOTES

1.

2.

3.

4.

MAY

15th

1. My **voice will speak** to your spirit when your heart is listening.

2. Your **victory for eternal life** happened on the cross.

3. Place each **hope and dream** in my hands so I may present them to the Father and ask to grant it according to His will.

4. Stay **connected to the vine** to stay connected to the father.

Memo Notes

1.

2.

3.

4.

MAY

16TH

1. The **breath of life** lives deep within you, use it purely.

2. Plant yourself into the heart of others. Let My **seed grow** as what has taken root in yours.

3. Never turn away your ear from a brother who is asking of your time. It **maybe I** who is doing the asking.

4. **Love of my life:** If you Love me as much as **I** love you, share with me everyone in your life.

MEMO NOTES

1.

2.

3.

4.

MAY

17ᵀᴴ

1. Let Me **shape your life** with confidence. Place all your thoughts in the Father's hand to bring about His will to your heart.

2. The **flesh will battle** your spirit continually. Put my defense of armor against the evil one.

3. Give to others what I have given to you: **love, mercy and forgiveness.**

4. **Each step** you take with Me will have a happy ending.

MEMO NOTES

1.

2.

3.

4.

MAY

18TH

1. Are you maturing in your walk **spiritually in Christ**?

2. I have **many children** but so few who will obey my teaching.

3. My love is never changing, even in **your disobedience** toward My word.

4. **Feel sorry** but pray for those who have taken advantage of your kindness.

Memo Notes

1.

2.

3.

4.

19TH

1. I prune you often to **bare fresh fruit** to share with others.

2. There is much more to **know about Me** than you will ever receive in this world.

3. It is time to move on from being fed raw milk into solid **foods to grow** spiritually and mature in Christ.

4. **Be a doer** of my word, plant seeds of me in everyone on your path.

Memo Notes

1.

2.

3.

4.

MAY

20TH

1. Show others **who I am**. Be an example of My love.

2. **Hand feed** all my children, for they do not know how to feed themselves of the Father's nourishment.

3. Be patient and **endure bad behavior**. Allow those who do not know me to speak their voice. Pray to me for their forgiveness.

4. Child, be filled with **life in Me**. It is plentiful.

Memo Notes

1.

2.

3.

4.

MAY

21ˢᵗ

1. Speak always **from the heart** what is shared, even to my children who stubble to listen.

2. **Let My will** be complied upon you in everything you ask and hope for.

3. Placed in your heart are **My wishes** from above. Reveal them and share with each other.

4. The Kingdom of Heaven is in **all My children**. All that is needed is an open heart to receive.

Memo Notes

1.

2.

3.

4.

MAY

22ND

1. It is the Father who sent Me. **Listen, trust** and **obey** what has been spoken.

2. My **children have much**. Is their thankfulness shared with the Father?

3. Everything in life is **God made**. The creator has given man his knowledge to create their needs.

4. Be **compassionate and caring** in doing My works.

Memo Notes

1.

2.

3.

4.

MAY

23ʳᵈ

1. **Steward My blessings** with thankfulness. Be grateful for all the Father has given.

2. Success in My children's lives is not how much you **accumulate**, but how much of your life of Me is shared with others.

3. A **created moment** is from the Father's wisdom planted in your heart.

4. Start **your day with Me.** End your day with Me and live your life with joy.

Memo Notes

1.

2.

3.

4.

MAY

24ᵀᴴ

1. Pray for the knowledge and **wisdom of the Father**. Open your heart to what you received and share with your brothers and sisters in Christ.

2. Let all that you seek to be a friend. Welcome them to **your best friend**.

3. **Align your life** with my word.

4. Give My children what is **shared with you**. My love, joy and kindness.

Memo Notes

1.

2.

3.

4.

MAY

25TH

1. Praying to Me is a must if you are planning to be a disciple of mine. I must **give direction first into** your heart.

2. All received from the Father is sent **from His authority** of whom He is.

3. **How is it** what my children have received becomes so forgetful of where it came from?

4. Are you a new **spiritual child** or born again in my son, Jesus Christ.

MEMO NOTES

1.

2.

3.

4.

MAY

26ᵀᴴ

1. I am your **Passover Lamb**.

2. **Hold nothing back** from your enemies. Share with them what I share with you. Treat them as your friend and not a stranger.

3. Slow down My children and be patient. Let My seed have its **harvest time** in your growth.

4. Give of self until **you have given your all**. No one has ever been hurt from a giver that gives everything of himself.

MEMO NOTES

1.

2.

3.

4.

27TH

1. My son's part is **finished,** your part has just begun.

2. Enjoy every day **with joy and laughter.** My kingdom is full of happiness that lasts forever.

3. **In you is Me.** In Me is you. What a beautiful relationship we share.

4. Kindness is a beautiful word. **Straight** with love **from the heart.**

Memo Notes

1.

2.

3.

4.

28TH

1. **Work is a mission field.** It is time for you to act out all your beliefs.

2. **Much grief** appears in my heart of those who deny who I am.

3. Loving someone **who loves you** back is easy, but loving someone who does not return it is a sacrifice.

4. Be of **good cheer, My child.** All that I share with you is from the Father's love of his children.

MEMO NOTES

1.

2.

3.

4.

MAY

29TH

1. **Life's purpose** is to have communication with me.

2. **Where you work.** I want my children to find meaning and purpose to express the Father's glory.

3. What you **receive in life** and what is shared back must not be compared. It is always better to give than receive.

4. All of life will have its share of **ups and downs**. Remember My love for you will never change.

Memo Notes

1.

2.

3.

4.

MAY

30TH

1. **Let no anger** gain strength in your heart that will turn away a brother or sister in Christ.

2. Each blessing the Father places in your life should be **cherished with thankfulness**.

3. **Let us pray together** and ask the Father for His provisions and protection in your walk.

4. I feed My sheep according to their needs. **Open** wide **your heart** to receive your portion.

MEMO NOTES

1.

2.

3.

4.

MAY

31ST

1. Fears of a **liar has death** written all over their heart.

2. In your heart is a **world full of My wisdom**. All that is needed to receive is prayer for the Father's will to be spoken.

3. **Be kind** to all in need, not out of man's pity!

4. **Feed My sheep daily.** Many of them will starve to death if left alone.

MEMO NOTES

1.

2.

3.

4.

June

JUNE

1ST

1. At your **family gatherings**, am I invited as one of your guest speakers?

2. It is in the **deep waters** of your storm where My work begins.

3. Do not judge **a know-it-all** brother. Ask then politely how much they know about Me.

4. Faith is not **positive thinking**. By faith is what the Father promises to do.

Memo Notes

1.

2.

3.

4.

JUNE

2ND

1. **Create a desire** in your life to obey Me by giving me all your heart.

2. The **stairway to Heaven** is only a prayer life away.

3. By faith in your spirit, allow yourself to receive what the **father is offering.**

4. You will rise again when My name is called out. **No more sorrow,** no more pain.

MEMO NOTES

1.

2.

3.

4.

JUNE

3ʳᵈ

1. In each of your lives lies a **hidden key** to My wisdom. All that is asked is for My children to unlock the opening to their hearts.

2. Turn away all hurts and anger in your heart. **Let nothing** conceive and overtake thee.

3. **Prosperity** is the makeup of your heart, share it with others.

4. As you **labor through life**, let all works be done for Me and for the glory of his name.

Memo Notes

1.

2.

3.

4.

JUNE

4th

1. Open the **doors of your heart** children to welcome the Father's ways to pass through.

2. All my **gifts from Heaven** are shared with all My children, but very few unwrap their hearts to receive them.

3. Let many of my words out of your heart be spoken to all **with love.**

4. Allow the one **who knows you best** to be received with gratitude and thanksgiving.

Memo Notes

1.

2.

3.

4.

JUNE

5TH

1. I show you **things of evil** to bring you back to Me that you may rest in the days of trouble.

2. All that has happened in the **past will return** if my children do not repent.

3. I am the Father of all **things on the earth** and of heaven. My ways are everlasting.

4. Trust in Me by faith. You will not survive on **man's promises**.

Memo Notes

1.

2.

3.

4.

JUNE

6ᵗʰ

1. Open your heart to be filled **with My Spirit**. Have none other enter.

2. Be careful what you allow in your heart. It may **grieve Me**.

3. Let all My sheep **graze in the fields**. Those who know Me when called will recognize and obey My voice.

4. The provisions needed for life are always available to those in need. The Father's house is a **storehouse of plenty**.

Memo Notes

1.

2.

3.

4.

JUNE

7th

1. **My children**, how much of your life is lived out for Me?

2. Sorry is a heart-warming word. **Forgive Me.**

3. Give to others a **portion of your heart**. Share with them what is Mine.

4. Only allow **interference** in your prayers when I begin to speak.

Memo Notes

1.

2.

3.

4.

JUNE

8TH

1. Children, I have so much to say and share with you. **Thank you** for taking the time to listen.

2. All my children who **believe in Me** will get fed daily, and those who choose not. All that I ask is to open your heart to receive much.

3. **Separation:** The price man will pay for denial of me.

4. As you **walk in the spirit**, your heart will be absent from the flesh.

Memo Notes

1.

2.

3.

4.

JUNE

9th

1. My child, you speak your heart of thoughts, I hear words of need. Are you **receiving My answers**?

2. Waste no time on self. Pursue your **pathway in Me**.

3. Remember, wherever **I lead you**, I am already there.

4. **Feed My sheep** with the Father's love. It is up to them to absorb it in their hearts.

Memo Notes

1.

2.

3.

4.

JUNE

10TH

1. I will not live in an **unclean body,** my child. All must be cleaned and purified for me to enter.

2. **Seeds unplanted** will never produce My crop.

3. Be a **spark of my likeness** wherever you glow.

4. No one will receive the **father's wisdom** unless it has been asked through me.

Memo Notes

1.

2.

3.

4.

JUNE

11TH

1. **Live your life righteously** so everyone will see My presence in you.

2. Let the stress in your life receive relief. **Read my word.**

3. What I accomplished in **thirty-three years** on earth was minimal to what My children are expected to produce.

4. How much of **your attitude** is spiritually fruitful?

MEMO NOTES

1.

2.

3.

4.

JUNE

12ᵀᴴ

1. How prosperous is a **wealthy man's life** without me?

2. Are you serving and craving for a Holy God that **fills your needs,** or a God who fills your wants that do not satisfy?

3. Leading My **sheep astray** will lead them to starvation.

4. Is living for Me **your priority,** or am I a back burner saved for last?

MEMO NOTES

1.

2.

3.

4.

JUNE

13TH

1. The Father always **keeps His promise** toward all His children. Are your promises worthy with others?

2. **Keep out** of your heart what is not mine.

3. All anger is not sinful, only that which causes you to take action **against your brother** or **sister.**

4. **How much truth** is planted in man's heart when I speak?

MEMO NOTES

1.

2.

3.

4.

JUNE

14TH

1. Man living without the Father's power will **walk a lifetime** in weakness.

2. Do not praise Me and curse your brothers and sisters. **Sinful anger** is never pleasing to the Father's will.

3. To live by faith in Me, you must be **trustworthy in your heart** in all I speak and do.

4. **Giving thanks for all** is a lifetime commitment if you're living your life for Me.

Memo Notes

1.

2.

3.

4.

JUNE

15ᵗʰ

1. Follow me in **all my ways** with forgiveness, compassion, and serving each other with the Father's love.

2. Let Me share someone I cherish dearly with you. My only **beloved Son, Jesus**.

3. **Hurry up my child.** Your life's too short without Me to please all your friends.

4. Share of Me this day to **become a spokesman** of the Father's word.

Memo Notes

1.

2.

3.

4.

JUNE

16TH

1. **Give your heart to all** as I have given my life for you.

2. Speak softly and gently to one another so **everyone will listen.**

3. **Follow me.** Those who follow me will always have a life preserver around their Hearts.

4. Feel the **compassion of My love** every time someone hugs you.

MEMO NOTES

1.

2.

3.

4.

JUNE

17th

1. Speaking from your heart **encourages others** to listen.

2. **Pretending** to be pleasant and not meaning it only deceives thyself.

3. Caring for all things that are received causes your **heart to care** for others in need.

4. Be a **listener from your heart** as the Father always listens to you.

Memo Notes

1.

2.

3.

4.

JUNE

18ᵀᴴ

1. All in My kingdom **care**.

2. Your time spent **doing my works** never becomes wasted only rewarded.

3. Sharing me can **become contagious.** Bring all of your friends to Me.

4. **Speak to me softly.** I am only a heartbeat away.

Memo Notes

1.

2.

3.

4.

JUNE

19ᵀᴴ

1. What has made your heart clean again? Nothing but the blood of **My Son, Jesus.**

2. I **pray for you, child,** that your faith does not fail you.

3. I am the **lighthouse of your heart**, always looking out ahead of your waters.

4. **Finish up My works** today. Tomorrow may never come to others.

Memo Notes

1.

2.

3.

4.

JUNE

20ᵀᴴ

1. My children, **stop keeping quiet** about my life. Have I not taught you my word must be shared?

2. I place many thoughts in your heart. **How many** do you live out for Me?

3. **There is nothing less** in the Father's heart than His love for you.

4. Be kind to your body. **Feed it my nourishment** daily.

MEMO NOTES

1.

2.

3.

4.

JUNE

21ST

1. I see so much joy in My children's heart as they receive a **gift from others**. How much more will they endure when I bring them home?

2. I give you **what you need** and not keep any for myself.

3. The Father wants all His children for Himself, make every day with Him **count**.

4. Overflow your life with the springs of **my living water**.

Memo Notes

1.

2.

3.

4.

JUNE

22ᴺᴰ

1. There is nothing in your life I consider useless, why are some of you **wasting it away**?

2. Occasionally, I will ask My children for their **stillness**. The Father has something to say.

3. What you **have in your heart** is more precious than silver or gold, the Father's love.

4. Show me how much you love me by **obeying his commandments.**

Memo Notes

1.

2.

3.

4.

JUNE

23RD

1. My time cannot hang on a wall. **It is timeless.**

2. Play Me over and over in your heart until you **memorize My love.**

3. **Proof to me** how much you love me by feeding my sheep.

4. How will My children ever get to know Me if they continue to **live for this world**?

MEMO NOTES

1.

2.

3.

4.

JUNE

24ᵀᴴ

1. Seek Me in the heart of others who are **searching for the Father's love**.

2. The life you live for Me will **never be disappointing**.

3. The **needy need my love,** share with them what I have shared with you.

4. Write down everything I ask. Then rewrite again **permanently in your heart**.

Memo Notes

1.

2.

3.

4.

JUNE

25ᵀᴴ

1. Be a **full-time spiritual worker**. No matter how part-time it may appear.

2. **Remind yourself** in the workforce who you are representing.

3. Questions unanswered. **Have you spoken to the Father lately?**

4. I share much with you because your **heart is listening**.

Memo Notes

1.

2.

3.

4.

26TH

1. **The kindness** in your heart, from where did that come?

2. The bible has one purpose, **The Glory of GOD!**

3. Take into your heart what **I am offering** with thanks.

4. All that is seen is by knowledge. All that is **unseen is by faith.**

Memo Notes

1.

2.

3.

4.

JUNE

27TH

1. Give **a heartful of thanks** to the Father for all He has given to you.

2. Speaking from the heart must always include the **Father's thoughts** in mind.

3. **Plan this day with** My Son, your Savior.

4. A leveled playing field is **two believing in Me**.

Memo Notes

1.

2.

3.

4.

JUNE

28TH

1. Be an **organ donor**. Give your heart away.

2. See me **smiling** when my children are sharing.

3. Never close the pages of your heart until I tell you, "it is finished."

4. **Speak My truth,** and no one may call you a liar.

Memo Notes

1.

2.

3.

4.

JUNE

29TH

1. When I say **peace be with you**, I also ask your heart to receive a piece of the Father's love.

2. **Customize your life** to match the Father's will.

3. Shed light that **reflects the Father's heart**.

4. Tomorrow will always come, with or **without me**.

MEMO NOTES

1.

2.

3.

4.

JUNE

30ᵗʰ

1. Place **no time clock** on the schedule I have given, see it through until completion.

2. Is there anything I could **say or do** for you that would be offensive?

3. Your words of mine shall **strengthen others** in their faith.

4. How foolish man has become to **judge my Truth**.

Memo Notes

1.

2.

3.

4.

July

JULY

1ST

1. **Did you know** that you alone may be the only believer to bring a child of mine to my son Jesus!

2. Each day is **a blessing** to whom you share your life with Me.

3. All children **separated from Me** head for departure.

4. You know me by my name, but do you **know me in your heart?**

Memo Notes

1.

2.

3.

4.

JULY

2ⁿᵈ

1. Praying for others should be part of your **everyday life with Me**.

2. "Temptation" is an **evil word** if carried through.

3. **Separate my thoughts** from those around you. My thoughts are not those of this world.

4. The **Lord is the Bible,** whether man believes GOD or not.

Memo Notes

1.

2.

3.

4.

JULY

3ᴿᴰ

1. Whatever is remaining in your life that is unclean, **dispose** of immediately.

2. Live your life without me, and your life will **pay the consequence.**

3. Come to Me before you **judge your brothers.** Take a deep breath and turn your cheek the other way.

4. **Sorrow**: I will **never desert** my children who cry out in times of trouble.

Memo Notes

1.

2.

3.

4.

JULY

4TH

1. I will never leave your heart empty, only fill you with My **Holy Spirit.**

2. **Life, love and family:** I have given you all from the Father's heart.

3. Following **footprints of My path** will lead you to the Father's righteousness.

4. Use your quill to **lead you to the pages** I have placed in your heart.

MEMO NOTES

1.

2.

3.

4.

JULY

5TH

1. Are you a **representative of Me** to your family and friends?

2. Where is your **patience with others**? Haven't I been patient with you?

3. Show others what **living for Me** brings into one's life.

4. Let My words speak to your **heart**.

Memo Notes

1.

2.

3.

4.

JULY

6ᵗʰ

1. **Life support**: My children, how much longer will I place your life on hold? I am here to offer salvation and make you whole again.

2. Give away **in your heart** what has been received by you.

3. Supplements are only worthy for the short term. **My nourishment is satisfying** forever.

4. Live each day for me. See how much happiness will become joy.

MEMO NOTES

1.

2.

3.

4.

JULY

7TH

1. Speak the truth about one another. Never deceive a brother with a **mouth full of lies**.

2. How much does your heart **live for Me**? Am I considered an insider or an outsider?

3. Go out **into the world** today, My child, share the Gospel and bring back souls for me.

4. **Tune the world out** and bring my life inside of yours.

MEMO NOTES

1.

2.

3.

4.

JULY

8TH

1. My child, allow My will to work in your life to **produce Godly fruit**.

2. Commit each day to **serve Me with much pleasure**.

3. Give thanks to the father for those children who come to me in time of need. I am **their healer and provider**.

4. Be **My peacemaker** to those who are angry with another.

MEMO NOTES

1.

2.

3.

4.

JULY

9TH

1. **You are so precious** in the Father's eyes. He only sees the beauty of His creation.

2. **Nurture your life** with My word until it is absorbed into your heart forever.

3. It is not enough to **reject sin,** but rejecting My word is life-threatening.

4. Listen to **my voice,** for it is easy to understand.

Memo Notes

1.

2.

3.

4.

10TH

1. There is **no Plan B** to enter my kingdom.

2. The glory of His being is His children, **a masterpiece** of Himself.

3. Think like me, child. **Look only at the beauty** in each of your brothers and sisters.

4. Have you **read about Me** this day?

MEMO NOTES

1.

2.

3.

4.

JULY

11ᵀᴴ

1. **It is I** whom speaks to your heart, and it is you who must listen.

2. Your **greatest weakness** will appear when your faith wanders away from my presence.

3. Have you **spoken to me lately?** The Father and I would love to hear from Our children.

4. I have filled **the pages to life**. Reading about Me will take a lifetime.

Memo Notes

1.

2.

3.

4.

12ᵀᴴ

1. Giving much is no different than to give less. What really matters is from **where it is coming.**

2. My spiritual treasures are all **My children**.

3. As you share your life with friends and family, may I become your **guest speaker?**

4. When others shut the door on Me, please **keep on knocking** until you receive an answer.

Memo Notes

1.

2.

3.

4.

JULY

13TH

1. Trust me by each step. **I am leading the way** to a place that I prepared for you.

2. Man will try to **scrub a dirt floor** without ever becoming clean.

3. Once you seek Me, you shall find Me. Your **heart will identify** the father, and your spirit will know him.

4. **Love all others** as I love them.

MEMO NOTES

1.

2.

3.

4.

14th

1. Children, **how does one prosper** who intentionally hurts another brother.

2. Listen to Me, trust Me, and obey My word, you will **never be disappointed**.

3. When others **draw to you**, they will also come to Me.

4. Remember, **when you pray to me**, the Father's heart hears your voice.

Memo Notes

1.

2.

3.

4.

JULY

15th

1. How easy for My children to become **burned out** and miss life's best.

2. Many things I want to **tell My children**, but only a few hearts are open to listening.

3. I am **with My children every** day and **every** night.

4. When you **give to others,** I am also receiving your gifts.

Memo Notes

1.

2.

3.

4.

JULY

16TH

1. All your life, I have been waiting for you to say to Me, "**Here I am, Lord!**"

2. Become **closer to me.** Hold in your heart thoughts of Me.

3. I am always here to **satisfy the thirst** of the heart, if you allow My hand to feed it.

4. There is only one cure for one who sins, **give your life** to my son Jesus Christ and ask for his forgiveness.

Memo Notes

1.

2.

3.

4.

JULY

17TH

1. Remember, **My thoughts** are not your thoughts but the ways of the Father.

2. **Friendly reminder.** Your citizenship is in Heaven. You are just passing through.

3. Store your **treasures in Heaven**. Earthly goods will soon disappear.

4. When you tell someone, "**I love you**," tell them you need them as well.

MEMO NOTES

1.

2.

3.

4.

18TH

1. Be thankful for not only this day. Be **full of thankfulness** for each day.

2. Let the Father **tenderize** your heart with His personal love and affection.

3. Do not **think** you will ever **outgrow** your love for me.

4. Enjoy the **light of each day** that shines in you with My presence that glows upon your walkway.

Memo Notes

1.

2.

3.

4.

19ᵀᴴ

1. When you **review your life** and need a change, do it before forgotten.

2. Growth in my spirit will **slow your anger**.

3. **Silence your tongue** to keep from backsliding in your spirit.

4. Continue in your faith in the direction **I am leading**.

Memo Notes

1.

2.

3.

4.

JULY

20ᵀᴴ

1. **I am the Lamb** on the cross that forgives all sin.

2. Thoughts of My Father: **Thanks-Given**.

3. The church is my temple, where My children gather to **worship me**.

4. **Death** will not claim those who follow me.

Memo Notes

1.

2.

3.

4.

JULY

21ˢᵀ

1. Every moment of your life with the father makes more **memories with Me**.

2. Be of good steward child. **Care for all** that has walked with me upon your road.

3. The luxury of **living for Me** is having everything in life worth living.

4. Let the **presence of Me be known** each time you enter your home.

Memo Notes

1.

2.

3.

4.

JULY

22ND

1. How much of your time do you spend **with your family** outside of the workplace?

2. **Amazing grace, how sweet it is!** Give thanks and praise to My Son Jesus for all his goodness.

3. **Contentment** makes a poor man's heart, rich.

4. Money is only a **season of joy**. This joy will not continue forever.

MEMO NOTES

1.

2.

3.

4.

JULY

23ʳᵈ

1. **How much do I love you,** child? Look what My Son suffered on the cross for you.

2. **Life's Work:** Man has a short time to work. Let it always be **Honoring the Lord.**

3. Love your neighbors, and give thanks! They are also your **brothers and sisters of mine**.

4. Give the father much pleasure by **reading his word**!

Memo Notes

1.

2.

3.

4.

24ᵗʰ

1. Follow My steps, children. **It will lead you to godly righteousness.**

2. **Invest in eternity,** share My Word with a friend.

3. Accept things as I see them. **Obey My thoughts,** child.

4. Be an **interpreter of Christ**. Share the Word.

Memo Notes

1.

2.

3.

4.

JULY

25TH

1. Let the heart only **speak with kindness and joy**.

2. Tell your **brothers and sisters** I am always with them.

3. Accept the will of the Father **ungrudgingly**.

4. **Convenience: It is easy** for your heart to find me.

MEMO NOTES

1.

2.

3.

4.

JULY

26TH

1. Greed, my son, leads to **one's disappointment**.

2. **Yes**, I depend on My children who know Me to love one another.

3. **The Father's wisdom** and knowledge come upon His children who spend their time with Him in prayer.

4. Remind yourself daily of **my presence** in your life.

Memo Notes

1.

2.

3.

4.

JULY

27TH

1. **Forgive others,** whether right or wrong.

2. Never worry about what **goes into your mouth**. Be aware of what may flow out.

3. Never think your **prayers are repetitious** when praying often. My heart takes them all in.

4. The peace you receive in your heart is joy. I will **sing to your soul**.

Memo Notes

1.

2.

3.

4.

JULY

28TH

1. **He claimed your destiny at calvary.**

2. There are no such things as **secret sins**.

3. **Hope:** Man does not always pray as he should **until** he is in need.

4. Many of my children **speak to Me each morning**, from many more, I would love to hear.

Memo Notes

1.

2.

3.

4.

JULY

29TH

1. There is no need to rush around in life when you are in **My time**.

2. Give someone something special from Me this day **your time**.

3. **Never allow** the needs of others to become hungry.

4. Children, if I can trust you with little, **much more** will be placed on your doorstep.

Memo Notes

1.

2.

3.

4.

JULY

30th

1. You cannot change man's heart that is **definable of My love**. Pray for them to repent of their thoughts.

2. Pray for the souls of others. Be a part of **my prayer team**.

3. **Child full of mercy**, pray My grace for those who refuse to accept Me.

4. All of my children who love me, know how to **Honor the Father**.

Memo Notes

1.

2.

3.

4.

JULY

31ST

1. Give thankfulness for the **little things in life**. Much happiness comes from this enjoyment.

2. Never cut apart what your Heart can untie, "**our relationship.**"

3. **Man's foolishness:** If you think GOD does not care about your problems, how is your Heart.

4. As a bird nurses its young, **feed My children's Heart** daily.

Memo Notes

1.

2.

3.

4.

AUGUST

AUGUST

1ST

1. I am in everything **that is** and always will be.

2. When a man sits on a throne that **does not belong to** him, his heart will become divided.

3. You're **allowing My thoughts** into your heart when you read and meditate upon each of my written words.

4. When your thoughts become big **enough to worry** about, it is time to pray for my answers.

MEMO NOTES

1.

2.

3.

4.

AUGUST

2ND

1. **Christ's return:** If you believe I will return without notice, clean up your life and **repent** before it is too late.

2. You are **poor spiritually** if you are missing the father's love in your heart.

3. Become a winner in the Father's eyes. **Never stop giving from** your heart.

4. **Only a few** will walk in the Father's pathway to Truth and eternal life.

Memo Notes

1.

2.

3.

4.

AUGUST

3ʳᵈ

1. I receive the **cry of the human heart**, but it does not always receive My response.

2. Is not my **life worth seeking** all of your time?

3. This world cannot satisfy a **hungry heart** for peace.

4. To those who **Walk in pride,** I am able to humble their Hearts.

Memo Notes

1.

2.

3.

4.

AUGUST

4TH

1. Do not become **slothful with your life as** it may lead to sin.

2. Let us speak daily to each other from our hearts. **Let us not become strangers**.

3. The busier your day, the more reason your life should **start each morning with prayer.**

4. When you tell your brothers in Christ that your time is available, **do you mean it** from your heart?

Memo Notes

1.

2.

3.

4.

AUGUST

5TH

1. **Continue to ask other**s how much they know Me.

2. One must **pray for My wisdom** before receiving its thoughts.

3. Listen from inside to **hear from above**.

4. Obeying the will of the Father is your responsibility for becoming a **doer of His word**.

MEMO NOTES

1.

2.

3.

4.

AUGUST

6TH

1. Fear not! **Walk with me.** The Father's hands are upon you.

2. To know me is to allow me to **Cross over your Borders** to enter your life.

3. Learn **how to listen** before speaking.

4. There is a lot more to **My book** than just reading it.

MEMO NOTES

1.

2.

3.

4.

AUGUST

7TH

1. My voice remains silent to those **hearts that remain closed**.

2. The **righteousness of the Lord** will one day cover the world and remove the sinner forever.

3. **Wait patiently** for My response. My timing is perfect.

4. You have of Me as much as **your heart desires**.

MEMO NOTES

1.

2.

3.

4.

AUGUST

8TH

1. Write **kindness in your heart**. There are no reasons for your heart to deny me.

2. I am **most satisfied** when My children read, obey, and share My word.

3. Let no days go by in your life without being a **representative of Me**.

4. **Blood at the cross:** The gospels are about my **Sacrificial Lamb** upon the cross.

MEMO NOTES

1.

2.

3.

4.

AUGUST

9TH

1. Be a **partnership for My children,** sharing everyone with me.

2. Show your employer you **can be trusted**. Recognize their authority and not be a complainer.

3. **Bring the truth** to your life. Live as I say.

4. **Listen**, **trust,** and **obey** everything written. Your life will change.

Memo Notes

1.

2.

3.

4.

AUGUST

10TH

1. My **rod of armor** is upon you. Be not afraid to speak My Truth. No one can harm you with the truth.

2. Show others that the life **that lives in you** is from above.

3. **Feed My sheep child**, let not one of them starve to death.

4. Children of Mine are **enemies of this world,** continually keep your faith upon me.

MEMO NOTES

1.

2.

3.

4.

AUGUST

11ᵗʰ

1. Your time on earth is short, but your time with Me **has no end**.

2. Many of My children are **aware of My name**, but very few know My heart.

3. There are **no holidays** from the will of God.

4. **My Word** is a miracle book and protector.

Memo Notes

1.

2.

3.

4.

AUGUST

12ᵀᴴ

1. I say **be on your guard** in a moment of weakness before sin overtakes your life.

2. The father created man for communication with me. Your **reward in heaven** reflects your obedience.

3. When someone questions My authority and asks for assurance, tell them **it is written**.

4. I repeat to you, **let not your heart** be troubled by what is spoken.

Memo Notes

1.

2.

3.

4.

AUGUST

13ᵗʰ

1. **Show your gratitude** toward Me. Share the Father's love with everyone.

2. Nothing you give **from your Heart** to my SON will ever be wasted.

3. Self is **not important** to the Father. Only your love for Him and others.

4. Are you enjoying life's journey with Me? **Why not invite others** to come.

Memo Notes

1.

2.

3.

4.

14TH

1. **No one** comes to Me unless the Father draws them My way.

2. Let each **challenge in your life** be of Mine.

3. **Do not become a judge** when someone you love fails you.

4. Allow each moment of suffering to be a **Lesson.**

Memo Notes

1.

2.

3.

4.

AUGUST

15th

1. Am I the **reason for all the seasons** in your life?

2. **To know Me this day** will not leave your heart empty tomorrow.

3. Marriage must have order: Husband, wife, and the Father **as one**.

4. **No one can hide** from my truth unless man refuses to believe that which is true.

Memo Notes

1.

2.

3.

4.

AUGUST

16TH

1. As a **wife serving your husband**, become a representative of Christ in his life.

2. My word is **not always what you want** to receive, but it is always what your heart needs most.

3. **False teachings:** If you see sheep eating other sheep, do not follow them. They are **raving wolves** in sheep clothing.

4. Are you **searching for answers?** Look no further than My word.

Memo Notes

1.

2.

3.

4.

AUGUST

17TH

1. A **thorn in the flesh** is sometimes needed to keep all eyes upon the Lord.

2. **Raise your children** from what is coming from within your heart.

3. Come worship and praise My Son. **Change your life forever.**

4. **Give to others** what their hearts are missing, a daily portion of Me.

Memo Notes

1.

2.

3.

4.

AUGUST

18ᵀᴴ

1. A **Heart filled with pride** could stop one from forgiving others.

2. Sow **that which you received** into other lives.

3. Fill your heart with Me, and I will fill your **life with my Father**.

4. Is your husband or wife at the **top of your prayer list?**

MEMO NOTES

1.

2.

3.

4.

AUGUST

19TH

1. Praying to Me takes focus off self and confusion. Place **everything in My hands.**

2. The **joy from above is what resides** in My children's hearts.

3. **No one** in Heaven has hate in their heart, that is simply nonexistent.

4. When you bring your child to a hospital **to be made whole,** let that child know who is performing the **Healing.**

Memo Notes

1.

2.

3.

4.

AUGUST

20TH

1. For the **inheritance** of cleansing, look on the CROSS.

2. Be careful of false teachers. Those who **know Me** may not follow Me.

3. What you know of the Father's Truth will **never leave you**.

4. I **never stop sharing** My heart with my children who are listening.

Memo Notes

1.

2.

3.

4.

21ST

1. Give the Father a gift of love, **your time**.

2. A **worthy walk with me** is pleasing to the Father's will.

3. Be in the **hall of faith** with me. Place your child in trust with me.

4. Did you know that when Mary kissed her baby, she had **kissed the face of our Lord?**

Memo Notes

1.

2.

3.

4.

AUGUST

22ND

1. A **Life without Me** is short and soon forgotten.

2. Healing this world of its **pain** and **suffering** is closer than ever before.

3. An ungodly man will not eat from a **good tree** that produces my fruit.

4. I will personally greet one who steps through My gate of Heaven.

Memo Notes

1.

2.

3.

4.

AUGUST

23ᴿᴰ

1. All I speak to your heart is true. **No one knows more** of the truth than the Father's son, who bears his name.

2. Many of My children have lost hope and faith to continue. Come to Me for **reasons to live a holy life** at its best.

3. **The seed of GOD** is within you, may it grow under his protection.

4. What you may think one can do in his strength, **bares no strength** at all.

Memo Notes

1.

2.

3.

4.

24ᵗʰ

1. I am **who I am** always!

2. I speak **nothing but the father's truth.** Let it remain in your thoughts forever.

3. **Where is Heaven?** In the believer's heart. Read all about it in my word.

4. **Compromising my word** is a sin against the father's authority.

Memo Notes

1.

2.

3.

4.

AUGUST

25th

1. Let the most significant part of your day **begin with Me**.

2. **Fill yourself** this day with Me. Fill it until it overflows with the **Father's Love**.

3. **The dead** have their **God,** Money possessions and little else. **The living will** have eternity and sharing of his Love **Forever!**

4. Everyone has the Father within him. Take time to **recognize His presence**.

Memo Notes

1.

2.

3.

4.

AUGUST

26ᵀᴴ

1. I ask all My children to live by My side, the **safety net** of his protection.

2. Those children who **Deny My Son** as Lord and Savior will soon discover their choice a life-threatening mistake.

3. Never let your heart become empty. Come daily for a fill of the **Father's nourishment**.

4. Go forth My child, **light up the Earth's** skies with Heaven shining upon you.

MEMO NOTES

1.

2.

3.

4.

AUGUST

27TH

1. Stay firm on the Father's schedule. His plan for your life is on **His time clock**.

2. Keep that **candle burning** in your Heart to follow the father and **me** to establish the walkway that leadeth to his pathway.

3. Are your labors through life for **Your Satisfaction,** or the Glory of His Kingdom?

4. **Everyday give thanks.** The Love of His heart grants you this day.

MEMO NOTES

1.

2.

3.

4.

AUGUST

28ᵀᴴ

1. **Store in your heart** each day the teachings of my being through every word.

2. When My children come to me with their Hearts open, I will **Come to them in the Spirit**.

3. Without being **Healed spiritually** physically has no meaning.

4. Treat others as I treat you, with both **love and compassion** without question.

Memo Notes

1.

2.

3.

4.

AUGUST

29ᵗʰ

1. The longer you listen, the more the Father **shares of His heart** with you.

2. My Son has given you His life, all the medicine you will ever need.

3. You are to **love your life** as I do.

4. **Turn your cheek away** from others as I have turned My heart away from your sins.

Memo Notes

1.

2.

3.

4.

AUGUST

30TH

1. To others, let them see a change in your life that they will **question why!**

2. Your **days on earth** will not last longer than I allow, use each moment wisely.

3. Drive out all fear in your life. **Place my promise** in your Heart to remove them all.

4. If a man lies to a brother, **who else hears him?**

Memo Notes

1.

2.

3.

4.

AUGUST

31ˢᵀ

1. All those **who have suffered** for the Father's sake await his reward in Heaven.

2. Lay down your life for your brothers and sisters. **Show thanks** for the Father's forgiveness of your sins.

3. You know My child **how to obey Me**. Live your life, according to my commandments.

4. In this world there will be uncertainty that no one will understand **except one**.

Memo Notes

1.

2.

3.

4.

September

SEPTEMBER

1ST

1. **Give Me your time,** and I will share with you all of My heart.

2. Set your life's pathway away from My Father and me, and I will **ignore your direction.**

3. Once you **commit your life** to Me, expect to live it for Me forever.

4. Looking **good on the outside** will never be satisfying enough to enter my kingdom.

Memo Notes

1.

2.

3.

4.

SEPTEMBER

2ᴺᴰ

1. Living on the **outside of my kingdom will** leave your life empty.

2. When you pray to the Father, **may I join you** in prayer?

3. Never rush when asked to wait. To Obey my answer and timing is always **made perfect.**

4. **Earthly riches** will one day disappear, but honoring My Word will lead to eternal blessing.

Memo Notes

1.

2.

3.

4.

SEPTEMBER

3ᴿᴰ

1. **I know** when you will tak your first step and when you will take your last. Let My Son take continuous steps in between.

2. Read about me daily, and your Heart will become **hungry no more**.

3. **MAN'S lost eternity** includes no Jesus, no Hope, and no Heaven. Welcome to the world of darkness.

4. I never allow blessings to My children who **take advantage** of those less fortunate.

Memo Notes

1.

2.

3.

4.

SEPTEMBER

4TH

1. Register your **life in Heaven**. Commit your life to My Son, Jesus Christ, to be accepted.

2. Who knows Me more than the Father? He **lives within Me**.

3. **What is in your heart?** That is full of Me.

4. My children praise Me when all is well. **Will they still praise Me** when I allow their life to be troubled for a season?

Memo Notes

1.

2.

3.

4.

SEPTEMBER

5ᵗʰ

1. **I always know** what you need before you ask. Bring your thoughts to me **by prayer.**

2. **Much more value.** Believe in Me and none of this world.

3. Notice all of Me in your life. **I am everywhere** you seek to find me.

4. Let go of the past and forgive those who have hurt you. **Forgiveness of others** is holy.

Memo Notes

1.

2.

3.

4.

SEPTEMBER

6th

1. **Claim everything I** share with you as truth.

2. When you get to where you are headed, **where will that lead you?**

3. Compromising My word will only **sadden your heart**.

4. **No one knows Me** Like the Father, except those who know the Father.

Memo Notes

1.

2.

3.

4.

SEPTEMBER

7ᵀᴴ

1. I am in the middle of your soul. I live in amid **your presence**.

2. **No one enters My gates** except those who give their hearts to My Son as their Lord and Savior.

3. If your Heart is a **stranger to prayer,** you will also be a stranger to my teachings.

4. **Jesus, My Son**, the perfect image of who **I AM.**

MEMO NOTES

1.

2.

3.

4.

SEPTEMBER

8TH

1. Happiness begins with those who **share My son** in self and with others.

2. **Do not become confused** about what you hear, but believe in what you have heard from above.

3. Search in your heart where I am lying. **I am No longer in a manger.**

4. Once My children **repent in their hearts**, I no longer remember their sin.

MEMO NOTES

1.

2.

3.

4.

SEPTEMBER

9TH

1. No one **mocks My children** that the Father does not despise.

2. Can anything compare to the richness of Heaven and spending **eternity with Me**?

3. **Compare yourself** with no one else except the Father.

4. I came into the world for just one purpose, to **save man's life.**

Memo Notes

1.

2.

3.

4.

SEPTEMBER

10TH

1. **Living with patience** is the absolute way to live out your life with me.

2. You may not know me, but **I know you well.**

3. One who listens to the Father **receives much wisdom** from above.

4. **Emptiness** in life becomes available in the absence of me.

MEMO NOTES

1.

2.

3.

4.

SEPTEMBER

11ᵀᴴ

1. To those who are dearest to your heart, **give them your time.**

2. **Do not nurse a grudge**, forgive your brothers and sisters.

3. **Half-hearted obedience** is disobedience in the Father's eyes.

4. Does your heart only hear the faults of others? Be like My son and Me, **forgotten.**

Memo Notes

1.

2.

3.

4.

SEPTEMBER

12th

1. I do not want half of your life. **I want it all** and all your time.

2. To those **ears that listen** from the heart shall receive much pleasure.

3. How much love **comes from above**? Everything the Father stores in his presence.

4. If you are not **Born again,** you will never enter the kingdom.

Memo Notes

1.

2.

3.

4.

SEPTEMBER

13ᵀᴴ

1. Experience not only happens in the classroom but also on **your Knee.**

2. **Come to me** to be free of your pain and be **free** of all your past hurts.

3. **Anxiousness** makes the heart grow weary.

4. There is nothing hidden from my eyes. **Think** before you commit that sin.

Memo Notes

1.

2.

3.

4.

SEPTEMBER

14TH

1. I am **never too busy** to hear the sounds your heart speaks.

2. Whatever your heart will say about Me, **believe it.**

3. The Bible has one purpose, and that is for **The Glory of God** to be shared.

4. **Excel** in your life. Walk daily in his holiness.

MEMO NOTES

1.

2.

3.

4.

SEPTEMBER

15ᵀᴴ

1. You have become **part of Me** as the Father has drawn your life to me. **He chose you.**

2. **My temple** is a hospital for all sinners.

3. A **need for salvation** leads to the service of others.

4. Be angered with a brother or sister, but **never dislike them**.

Memo Notes

1.

2.

3.

4.

SEPTEMBER

16ᵗʰ

1. Be an **encouraging disciple** wherever the Father leads you.

2. Are you part of **My daily plan**, or others?

3. You do not know **when I shall return**. Live it expectedly this day.

4. My spiritual children are **ordinary people** that became holy and lived by my teachings.

Memo Notes

1.

2.

3.

4.

SEPTEMBER

17ᵀᴴ

1. As you **share your thoughts** with Me, the Father listens with anxiousness.

2. You ask Me to speak. I have spoken, **read My word**.

3. Man has little hope on his own. There's **hope given freely** through me.

4. **Leave life alone!** I created all things in My image for all of man's joy.

Memo Notes

1.

2.

3.

4.

SEPTEMBER

18ᵀᴴ

1. If I have saved your life, it was **worth dying for.**

2. **Love one another** for the sake of loving Me and the Father.

3. Place in your heart the things of above. **They never become old!**

4. Continue to create in your heart **a home for Me.**

Memo Notes

1.

2.

3.

4.

SEPTEMBER

19TH

1. **Give of thyself** all that there is!

2. Living in My world can only bring **happiness** found in no other place.

3. Continuous sinning will **remove my Blessings.**

4. You can be **near to me,** but you may not be **in me.** Lose yourself into my presence.

Memo Notes

1.

2.

3.

4.

SEPTEMBER

20TH

1. **Listening to Me** speaks for itself.

2. No one knows the Father except Me. **Get to know Him** through Me.

3. **Say no to God,** and your children may also suffer.

4. Be as **important to others** as important as I became to you.

Memo Notes

1.

2.

3.

4.

SEPTEMBER

21ST

1. How safe are you without **My arms around you**?

2. When I **Challenge your walk,** it is not of harm but a test of trust and faith toward me.

3. My children **know the truth,** but many refuse to accept it.

4. The love for my children grows and **never diminishes** because of their sins.

Memo Notes

1.

2.

3.

4.

SEPTEMBER

22ᴺᴰ

1. **Savior:** Search for my children whom became lost in their life and bring them back home to me.

2. I have **written my life** in your heart. Listen for me to reveal it.

3. Serving me is a commitment of trust **and proving your faith.**

4. **I love you** ,child. You are a listener of Mine.

Memo Notes

1.

2.

3.

4.

SEPTEMBER

23ᴿᴰ

1. **Be Me** in your walk. All will ask questions.

2. It is **from my Heart** I speak and no other place.

3. **Positive thinking** without my instructions is only a thought.

4. I ask not to receive back what I have shared with you, I only **ask of your life**.

Memo Notes

1.

2.

3.

4.

SEPTEMBER

24ᵗʰ

1. My child **be Christ-like** in everything you do.

2. **Have much to be said?** Let it be spoken. I am listening.

3. The most important thing you can give in life is your time. **Give it generously**.

4. **No sorrow or pain** may approach you unless the father allows it for a purpose in your life.

Memo Notes

1.

2.

3.

4.

SEPTEMBER

25ᵀᴴ

1. My children, **in all your weakness** may you find my strength beyond measure.

2. **A moment in time** life will have left you, think before you deny me.

3. Bring love to **someone's home.** Share me as family.

4. You will have many friends, but I will remain **your best friend forever.**

MEMO NOTES

1.

2.

3.

4.

SEPTEMBER

26th

1. **True contentment in me** takes you off self.

2. I send blessings to all My children. All receive sunshine and all receive rain, but **those lives given to Me** will spend life in eternity forever.

3. Obedience to Me is **non-negotiable**.

4. To **share Me,** you must first get to know Me.

Memo Notes

1.

2.

3.

4.

SEPTEMBER

27TH

1. Cautiously you speak about me, **can anyone recognize the truth?**

2. Come to my Temple to **Praise and Honor** the Father and to receive his teachings.

3. Never fight life's trials alone. **This is your Father speaking.**

4. **Godly living** is how I see my children's lives.

Memo Notes

1.

2.

3.

4.

SEPTEMBER

28ᵀᴴ

1. Participate in your marriage. Be full of Me for each other. **Marriage is a sacred commitment.**

2. I am **full of life**. Come share it with the one who lives it every day in heaven.

3. The Father holds back nothing for Himself. **Everything is shared** and given to His children.

4. Because you chose to live for me, your life must **never be denied with others.**

Memo Notes

1.

2.

3.

4.

SEPTEMBER

29ᵗʰ

1. Let my Spirit be a **councilor to your heart.** The Father's wisdom applies.

2. I will always respond **by your Faith** in me.

3. **Think about it first!** Everything I place into your heart has been written.

4. **My house:** When you come to my Temple, I am not begging for money, only your heart.

Memo Notes

1.

2.

3.

4.

SEPTEMBER

30TH

1. Owning a lot will not bring satisfaction. Come to me and I will **share the Father's** Love to satisfy.

2. You think you can hide your life from the Father and me, think twice. **We are everywhere.**

3. None of my children were **created** without purpose, ask in prayer to reveal your calling.

4. **Doubting faith** is not of me.

Memo Notes

1.

2.

3.

4.

October

OCTOBER

1ˢᵀ

1. I am enough. I always will be. Be satisfied with what is **in your heart**.

2. **Hear the beauty** of the singing birds, feed your heart with the beauty of their songs.

3. **No one** can deny that I am who **I AM** if they know me in the spirit.

4. I am your loving Father. You are **My loving children**.

Memo Notes

1.

2.

3.

4.

OCTOBER

2ᴺᴰ

1. Nothing has **more value in your life** than to share the Father's heart with My children.

2. Some of My children may not know Me, but **I know them well**.

3. Every room at the **Inn of Heaven is open**. No doors will ever be closed to those who knock!

4. Where does lying take you? **Straight into the entrance of Hell**.

Memo Notes

1.

2.

3.

4.

OCTOBER

3rd

1. **Speak to my children** with kindness and gentleness. Many of my children have broken lives. They need to share someone who knows the Father's love.

2. When you **hear My voice,** you may forget it soon, but I placed what has been heard in your heart forever.

3. Prepare your heart in my word, trouble may approach **without an invitation.**

4. A Christian in need? Ask a **brother in Christ**.

MEMO NOTES

1.

2.

3.

4.

OCTOBER

4TH

1. In my Kingdom, **those hearts that were broken** will become whole.

2. Share with others what you have received from **the Father's Spirit**.

3. **Knowledge upon your heart** has been placed according to my Father's will.

4. Place what the Father reveals in a keepsake **stored in your heart** forever.

Memo Notes

1.

2.

3.

4.

5ᵗʰ

1. **Earthly Meltdown**: Read all about it in Revelation.

2. How defiant My children have become that **they must always learn the hard way.**

3. Never worry about Me not caring, **I care for everyone.**

4. More important than work and possessions, is your **time spent with each other** praying.

Memo Notes

1.

2.

3.

4.

OCTOBER

6ᵀᴴ

1. Learn and discipline yourself to be **satisfied with less.** You will be much more content.

2. **Never be judgmental** of others, only a comforter to their needs.

3. Let those who cannot see, **see.**
   Let those who cannot hear, **hear.**
   Let your spirit in Me receive **ALL.**

4. The lessons you learn today will **provide wisdom** for tomorrow.

MEMO NOTES

1.

2.

3.

4.

OCTOBER

7TH

1. You may have **religion in your life,** but do you have my son, Jesus?

2. **Never force** upon your heart those things that are not from above.

3. Sharing one another's burdens is an **act of your love** towards me.

4. No day could ever be lost that has been **shared with Me.**

MEMO NOTES

1.

2.

3.

4.

OCTOBER

8TH

1. Child, when you **teach your children** right from wrong, do you also teach them by My word?

2. What is your rush? Have I not **satisfied your hungry heart**? Let My word be digested.

3. Those who you cared about in the past but never see, **keep on caring** for them in prayer.

4. I ask that you **honor My Son** with all your heart and with all your life. He deserves both.

MEMO NOTES

1.

2.

3.

4.

OCTOBER

9TH

1. Man does not impress the Father when man **does not share** what He has received.

2. Live a life where **giving of self** is always your first thought.

3. **Sit tight and wait** for my answer. It will never be late.

4. **Guard your faith** against anxiety and protect it with your mind upon me.

Memo Notes

1.

2.

3.

4.

OCTOBER

10TH

1. Mercy is an **act of my Father's will**. Few know where it came from.

2. Connection with the Father and Me will always be a **three-way street**.

3. A moment each day with me could lead to a **lifetime with the Father**.

4. Laziness is not accepted as **Godliness**.

MEMO NOTES

1.

2.

3.

4.

OCTOBER

11TH

1. Bring **no one into My house** that cares for only thyself.

2. **Creation:** In me all things are held together. **I spoke** the world into **existence.**

3. Be **careful how you share Me**. Some will accept Me because they know Me, while others will reject Me because they do not.

4. **Separate Me** in your heart and away from this world.

MEMO NOTES

1.

2.

3.

4.

OCTOBER

12ᵀᴴ

1. **Loving your enemies** will not end their lives.

2. Sharing, **how much caring** does it cost?

3. Who is **wearing the pants** in your life? The Father or self?

4. My child, exhaust in Me in prayer. No one can **satisfy the heart** as I.

MEMO NOTES

1.

2.

3.

4.

OCTOBER

13ᵗʰ

1. Do not try to bring My lost children **out of the desert** overnight. Many have been there for most of their lives.

2. The **Father knows the hearts** of all His children. Not one is misplaced.

3. Life's certainties are always changing unless they are **in My hands**.

4. The **foundation of Christ** is within you.

MEMO NOTES

1.

2.

3.

4.

OCTOBER

14ᵀᴴ

1. Do not become a **Speak-alcoholic** when listening to the Father's voice.

2. Whom you live for, is **whom you will serve**.

3. **Easy-living** is what my Father offers.

4. My children, **be full of me**, for I am full of the Father's love.

Memo Notes

1.

2.

3.

4.

OCTOBER

15TH

1. **Be sensitive** to My teachings. Every spoken word has a meaning.

2. Always pray until I **answer.**

3. Center your heart on My Son Jesus and you will **never lose focus** of your life.

4. **Kindness costs** so **little**. All can afford it.

MEMO NOTES

1.

2.

3.

4.

OCTOBER

16ᵀᴴ

1. Peace I give you. Have you lately **shared** it **with your enemies**?

2. Discipline your soul with the **Father's righteousness**.

3. Keep My connection Gate wide open for it is **charged with life**.

4. What happens when My children listen to me**? ALL is Good.**

Memo Notes

1.

2.

3.

4.

OCTOBER

17TH

1. Raise up your **hands in praise**. All is recorded in the Father's heart.

2. I love My children who **give back to me**. I grieve those children who keep all for themselves.

3. Be obedient to the Father's Word and receive your **rewards in Heaven**.

4. Spending **time on your knees** will distract your life from becoming like the world.

Memo Notes

1.

2.

3.

4.

OCTOBER

18TH

1. Always receive **sanctification on your knees.** Pray until your heart becomes cleansed.

2. Allow My Holy Spirit to fill your thoughts. Be a **model of the Father's will.**

3. Evil thoughts will divide your mind in **times of Weakness.**

4. Is your church **multiplying spiritually** to fulfill His kingdom with His children?

MEMO NOTES

1.

2.

3.

4.

OCTOBER

19TH

1. Do your **works in My Spirit**, not of your flesh.

2. Live each day as I am **living in you**.

3. If you want to give something to others that is pleasing to the Father, **give more of self**.

4. **Body of Christ:** My children, called out of this world, will become part of my family in Christ.

MEMO NOTES

1.

2.

3.

4.

OCTOBER

20ᵀᴴ

1. Your heart is full of many wonders. The **wonder of truth** is My word.

2. Failure will come to My children's lives when they **walk out on Me**.

3. My will must be your will. **Separate self** from this world and obey me.

4. Sin is **Lawlessness!** Look around you to find chaos in your unbelieving brothers.

Memo Notes

1.

2.

3.

4.

21ˢᵗ

1. Whatever I share with you, take it with **thanks**.

2. **Be patient** with what you hear said of me to others. It takes time for many to know Me.

3. The Father and I share the same visions. **The Father and I are one.**

4. Be more concerned of **what you can give** of yourself than what may be received.

Memo Notes

1.

2.

3.

4.

OCTOBER

22ᴺᴰ

1. My will for your life does not have to **remain a mystery**, read my word to understand.

2. **"Creator":,=** I am not only your creator, but I am also the **sustainer** of life.

3. Work for God in your heart, **not for man.**

4. **Never compromise** My will. Nothing is further from the truth.

MEMO NOTES

1.

2.

3.

4.

OCTOBER

23RD

1. Prayer will never change Me. It will only **change lives.**

2. Become a part of the **Father's welcoming committee.** Invite everyone into your heart to meet with me.

3. **Illuminate my word and** live out my instruction book.

4. **Weep, My Son,** for those hearts that deny living by my word. Their destiny will soon come to an end.

MEMO NOTES

1.

2.

3.

4.

OCTOBER

24ᵀᴴ

1. **Change your heart.** Change your life.

2. Works **without prayer** make man's heart weak.

3. The Father and **I never sleep.** In Heaven, all are awake.

4. Let **his Grace** take each day upon you.

Memo Notes

1.

2.

3.

4.

OCTOBER

25TH

1. I can only bring to you that **shared through Me.** You must bring yourself to the Father to receive what He has given through Me.

2. Unless it is read and lived, you will forget it. **My words lead to everlasting life.**

3. Hope always **knocks at your door.** Open your heart to receive Me.

4. **Remember that My Sabbath** is a day of rest in Me.

MEMO NOTES

1.

2.

3.

4.

OCTOBER

26ᵀᴴ

1. You build My temple in your heart, and I will protect you with My wall. **You have My promise.**

2. If not of My timing, it is **time to wait** until instructed.

3. It is up to you to carry **through My works**. I will be with you until you finish.

4. **Selfish living** begins when waiting on my timing to expire in your patience.

Memo Notes

1.

2.

3.

4.

OCTOBER

27TH

1. **Speaking truth,** not lies will honor the Father's will.

2. If His path guides your heart, it is natural to walk in the ways of the Father.

3. Praise the Father and Me as **your keeper** and provider. We should be your life support.

4. I write in your heart what you need, not what you want. **The Father and I** are your caretakers.

MEMO NOTES

1.

2.

3.

4.

OCTOBER

28TH

1. It is **time to share** what was written.

2. The **battlefield of sin** begins in the mind.

3. My **promise book** is like none found anywhere else.

4. Come let us **adore My Son.** He has much to be praised for.

Memo Notes

1.

2.

3.

4.

OCTOBER

29ᵀᴴ

1. Your motives must be **honoring and pleasing** to the Father in all that you do and say.

2. Discover why I love you as I do. **Read My Word.**

3. **Without holiness** in your life, you will not recognize Me.

4. The **richness in life** begins with Me.

Memo Notes

1.

2.

3.

4.

30ᵀᴴ

1. Manage My truth to the fullest. **Be a steward** of what I have entrusted into your life.

2. Rushing through life: Where does that take you? **No place but confusion.**

3. Protect your integrity. Get it right with the Father. **Walk with His righteousness.**

4. **Man's choice:** Giving in to sin is not a choice at all. Lay it down before it takes over your life.

Memo Notes

1.

2.

3.

4.

OCTOBER

31ST

1. The spoken truth is **My Word**

2. All of Me is within you. **Allow no days** to pass by without speaking to Me.

3. I am the Father, the Son, and the Holy Spirit. Each day in your life **depends on all of Me**.

4. Time to wake up My child, time to **arise for Jesus**.

MEMO NOTES

1.

2.

3.

4.

November

NOVEMBER

1ST

1. How much of Me is known in your heart? **Do you really know who I am?**

2. **Sacrificial offering** was taken to the cross for all My children.

3. I do not speak to your heart to be **unheard**.

4. What you are willing to die for you should also be **willing to live for.**

Memo Notes

1.

2.

3.

4.

NOVEMBER

2ᴺᴰ

1. **Through my children:** Speak more of me and less of man.

2. When you bring **yourself to me** in prayer, your heart must be willing to wait for my answers.

3. Stop trying to avoid Me. **Man cannot live** life without Me.

4. **Compromising my word** for others will only sadden your heart.

Memo Notes

1.

2.

3.

4.

3ʳᵈ

1. Let not your Heart become discouraged with my direction. **Read what has been spoken** until it has taken root in your Heart.

2. **Temporary faith** is never lasting.

3. Invest in others. **Spend quality** time with your brothers and sisters in prayer.

4. **False teachers** smell like sheep. They shave your wallets to fill their needs.

Memo Notes

1.

2.

3.

4.

NOVEMBER

4TH

1. Let it be known in your life. **Heaven or Hell**, you make your choice.

2. **Unity with Christ**: Security is not in man's work. No one lives forever of his own free will.

3. Give what has been spoken to others **with authority**. It is not to be taken lightly.

4. My wisdom **surprises others** who do not know Me.

MEMO NOTES

1.

2.

3.

4.

NOVEMBER

5TH

1. You seek Me, you find Me, **here I am child!"Here I am Child."**

2. **God's provisions:** Count all your Blessings before you lay your head to rest.

3. Do not allow the **sparkle of life** to ever leave you, **My Son**.

4. **I** am completely man and completely **God.** This is who I am!

MEMO NOTES

1.

2.

3.

4.

NOVEMBER

6ᵀᴴ

1. Be that **missing link** to someone who needs to receive the LORD.

2. I am easy to find. You never have to look far away. **I will just appear.**

3. **Wait for guidance** in your footsteps. I know what steps you need to take first.

4. No greater a gift that pleases the Father than the gift of **giving of self** to others.

Memo Notes

1.

2.

3.

4.

NOVEMBER

7ᵀᴴ

1. **Denial of my Son:** No one can wash you from my hands unless one's Heart refuses to be held.

2. Be like the **root of a tree** in your faith. Stay focused on the growth of its leaves.

3. If your schedule becomes ahead of mine, **stumbling awaits you.**

4. Man has taken what was made for good and remade into evil, a **deceiving heart** of my works.

Memo Notes

1.

2.

3.

4.

NOVEMBER

8ᵗʰ

1. Who is your **best friend** when all others fail you?

2. All Earthly **treasures are meaningless** without Me.

3. **In Man's weakness** is the Father's strength.

4. **Wavering faith** always leads to disappointment.

Memo Notes

1.

2.

3.

4.

NOVEMBER

9th

1. My children if I wrote a book about Heaven it would be titled: **Without Ending.**

2. **My Word:** Directions for all man's life.

3. I came into a **broken world** to mend your broken hearts.

4. **Contentment with the Lord** surpasses all pleasures of man's Heart.

Memo Notes

1.

2.

3.

4.

NOVEMBER

10ᵀᴴ

1. The life of the Father and I **is sacred.** All our children are asked to share it with us this day.

2. Consider bringing to your life all things from above. **Consider them all good.**

3. Applying my thoughts to your heart will bring **wisdom** to one's heart that is listening.

4. **Mistreating others** is displeasing to the Father and upsetting to his children.

Memo Notes

1.

2.

3.

4.

NOVEMBER

11TH

1. **Fellowship of Love,** join me each morning in prayer.

2. If you want to write a book, write a story of your **life shared with me.**

3. **My will be done** on Earth as in Heaven, or man's life will be removed from him forever.

4. How satisfied are those who **give their hearts** away?

MEMO NOTES

1.

2.

3.

4.

NOVEMBER

12ᵀᴴ

1. How little time it takes to imitate the Father's love, **your whole life**.

2. Clearly, I say to you, love My children with all your heart, all your soul and with **all My love**.

3. Remind yourself daily, **whose life you are representing**?

4. No one, My child, has more **love to give** than the Father himself.

Memo Notes

1.

2.

3.

4.

13ᵀᴴ

1. Everything spoken from above is **worthy of Hearing** and living for the truth.

2. No one in Heaven spends time alone. We are one **big family in love** with one another.

3. In my Holy Spirit are many **Wonders proclaiming the truth.**

4. You will never have full contentment until you walk in the **Light of my Son,** Jesus Christ.

Memo Notes

1.

2.

3.

4.

NOVEMBER

14ᵀᴴ

1. Come to Me with saddened hearts and I will make them **disappear**.

2. Seek Me out when most **dissatisfied with self.**

3. **Unbelievers:** Chasing life outside my will causes man to follow promises that do not exist.

4. **Keep Me coming** into your life and I will never stop to rest.

Memo Notes

1.

2.

3.

4.

NOVEMBER

15ᵀᴴ

1. I am all the time, **all the time with you.**

2. **The pages of My life** will never have an ending.

3. **You are a listener** of mine. Be a doer of My word.

4. Creation: **one child at a time.**

MEMO NOTES

1.

2.

3.

4.

NOVEMBER

16ᵀᴴ

1. **How much of Me** can you stand? The Father and I hope all.

2. **Notify Me** when your heart is acting up.

3. Do not take my children from **My Temple, for** those who deceive them from my word will pay a penalty.

4. Fetch My children **out of the sea** before they become like the dead sea.

Memo Notes

1.

2.

3.

4.

NOVEMBER

17ᵀᴴ

1. Is there anything that my heart could say to you that would **offend you**?

2. When I place your **life on pause,** it is for my purpose to teach the Heart more patience.

3. You are always right until your heart **hears My truth.**

4. Are any of My children **unrelated to the Father**?

Memo Notes

1.

2.

3.

4.

NOVEMBER

18ᵀᴴ

1. Remove your troubled heart from worries, focus **your life on my promise**.

2. Be thankful for the little things in life. Without man's knowledge **from the Lord** nothing would exist.

3. **Water the soil** of your heart with My word.

4. My wisdom is **made perfect**. Available for all who are seeking.

---◆---

Memo Notes

1.

2.

3.

4.

NOVEMBER

19ᵀᴴ

1. Once your Heart has been given to me, your life will **never stay the same.**

2. My word is full of wisdom. It **must be asked for** in order to create great things.

3. You are not living for this world, but you live among it. **Represent Heaven's way.**

4. **Chase my peace.** It will not come on its own.

MEMO NOTES

1.

2.

3.

4.

NOVEMBER

20ᵗʰ

1. **Weep with your brothers** who are weeping, and share man's sorrows.

2. The condition of My church **has become poor.**

3. **My protection:** Remember your past when times of worry were real. What has become of them?

4. The luxury of living for Me: **Heaven awaits you.**

Memo Notes

1.

2.

3.

4.

NOVEMBER

21ˢᵗ

1. **Life's safety check:** How much time in prayer is spent with the **Father** each day.

2. **Keep life simple.** Relate all life's worry under my protection.

3. Write as I speak. **Do as I say.**

4. Do not speak My **words in riddles**. No one will understand.

Memo Notes

1.

2.

3.

4.

22ᴺᴰ

1. I am so excited to **share My thoughts** with you I could not hold back another word.

2. **Accountable Truth:** Every child will stand before my son in **Judgment.** Prepare your Heart for this time of truth.

3. The Father **will not speak** to His children if He has nothing to say.

4. When trouble comes to your marriage, **come to my church** for his answer.

Memo Notes

1.

2.

3.

4.

NOVEMBER

23RD

1. As a believer in Christ, always remember I am the one **leading the way.**

2. I can provide what all My children need with certainty. Life **contentment with Me.**

3. Look for Me in your workplace. **How convenient** I am.

4. Do not let the enemy twist your thoughts. **Stand firm on My Word.**

Memo Notes

1.

2.

3.

4.

NOVEMBER

24ᵀᴴ

1. **Speak clearly and patiently** from the heart. Many more will listen.

2. Feed your heart My fruit and vegetables from Heaven. **See what becomes** of you**r life.**

3. I can **change your circumstances** in a moment's thought. Pray to me often.

4. **Invest in this day** with your works for the Lord. His pay is always rewarding.

Memo Notes

1.

2.

3.

4.

NOVEMBER

25TH

1. **There is more of Me** than what has been spoken.

2. You can make mistakes. You will be forgiven when you **repent of your sin** to My Son, Jesus Christ.

3. Let my **instruction book** be removed from your life and miss God's best.

4. **Do not give up on Me.** No one has ever succeeded without Me.

MEMO NOTES

1.

2.

3.

4.

NOVEMBER

26ᵀᴴ

1. No man escapes **death**, the Gospel is your Good News.

2. It is **what you need** that I have given before you have asked.

3. Tell me you **love Me with all your heart and** show Me by sharing this love with others.

4. Doing only good will never pass on God's **Judgment day.**

Memo Notes

1.

2.

3.

4.

NOVEMBER

27ᵀᴴ

1. **Wavering faith** causes man to think. **I hope so!**

2. Be not angry with **the world's answers**. They are only temporary.

3. The light of the world is upon those who **travel after me** in their Hearts.

4. Always give whatever you can, but **apply its truth from your heart**.

Memo Notes

1.

2.

3.

4.

NOVEMBER

28TH

1. **Heartaches**, not where my home resides.

2. **Definite Request** for answers begins on your knees.

3. Nothing from My Word will ever become old and forgotten. Only those **hearts that turn away** from it.

4. Never ask me for a reason to sin. **I will never answer.**

Memo Notes

1.

2.

3.

4.

NOVEMBER

29TH

1. Let the **light of My Son** shine through you. Never allow darkness to shine anywhere in your life.

2. **Man's Future occupancy**: Heaven or hell.

3. Every moment your heart reveals **thoughts of Me**, the fonder your heart becomes to obey the Father's will.

4. **Kindness costs** so little. Share it and show it always.

MEMO NOTES

1.

2.

3.

4.

NOVEMBER

30ᵀᴴ

1. **The works I did** on Earth were minimal. I go to the Father to ask of your works to become greater.

2. **A servant Master:** The servant must be like his master, serve my children as a shepherd to lead the Father's sheep.

3. All things given from above have been **given freely**. Why not share my blessings with others.

4. The Spirit of Truth **comes from within** and received from above.

MEMO NOTES

1.

2.

3.

4.

December

DECEMBER

1ˢᵀ

1. Let others know what the **Father has done** in your life **for you.**

2. **Join Me in prayer** each morning. We have much to share with each other.

3. What else can I say to your heart that will **make you listen** more.

4. **Short term memory.** I hope not of Me.

Memo Notes

1.

2.

3.

4.

DECEMBER

2ND

1. **Finding yourself all** alone is your choice.

2. No one should live his **life journey** without Me, only those who choose.

3. When **patience fails you,** turn to me for calmness.

4. Where am I? Heaven. Where have you come from? Heaven. Where will you live together with me forever? **In Heaven.**

MEMO NOTES

1.

2.

3.

4.

December

3rd

1. You have **God's charm** because you have all I am.

2. My **children's lips** speak well of Me, but many hearts rebuke to not know Me more.

3. Look at My children with love in your heart, not **lust of their flesh**.

4. **Be Praiseworthy:** Much joy comes to my children who worship and **praise the Lord** together at his Holy temple.

Memo Notes

1.

2.

3.

4.

DECEMBER

4TH

1. **Empty church**, are you one of My missing children?

2. Be a **teacher of My Word.** Exploit it with one another.

3. **Love of Christ:** It will become a losing situation to those who try to hide away from my Love.

4. Your heart can speak on its own. Has it **spoken to the Father** lately?

MEMO NOTES

1.

2.

3.

4.

DECEMBER

5TH

1. If you trust me with your life, you will **never be ashamed of** what has been written.

2. **God's glory:** Those who respond to my word may your life be placed upon his Glory.

3. Am I **filling the pages** to your heart? Keep it open to receive its meaning.

4. In my word is where you will **meet my son, JESUS!**

Memo Notes

1.

2.

3.

4.

6TH

1. Who ever said I am **Heaven sent!**

2. Create a moment and **think of Me often**.

3. Use all my words to be your lens to **View the World**.

4. **Let us search** in your heart for what I am looking for.

Memo Notes

1.

2.

3.

4.

DECEMBER

7ᵀᴴ

1. **Ancient history**, how it repeats itself.

2. **Tolerating man's sin** is no excuse to accept it.

3. So many of My children need My help. **Shame on them** for not asking.

4. What brings your heart to Me, could it be **My love?**

Memo Notes

1.

2.

3.

4.

8ᵗʰ

1. If I be **brought into your life,** I will bring much more into yours.

2. My world is becoming like a **Deserted Island,** living without my word.

3. No one **wants the truth.** Look how few are listening to my teachings.

4. Worship has never been a choice, **only God's command.**

Memo Notes

1.

2.

3.

4.

DECEMBER

9TH

1. Share no evil **in Heaven**.

2. Everyone could use a **helping hand**. Why not ask for Mine?

3. I load up your heart with many of his thoughts. **Enjoy them daily.**

4. How particular are you with your life? **I am also particular** with your life.

Memo Notes

1.

2.

3.

4.

10ᵀᴴ

1. Where will life lead you **without Me**?

2. **Leadership in My church**, are you part of its growth?

3. How would you like to **know Me infinitely**? Let us pray together on our knees and speak to the father.

4. **Quiet times** alone with Me is such a beautiful memory.

Memo Notes

1.

2.

3.

4.

DECEMBER

11ᵀᴴ

1. Is your church **centered by the Father's word?**

2. **Disciple one another.** Encourage each other with the Father's will from your hearts.

3. **Cling to me** when trouble approaches your life.

4. A messenger of Mine may appear to you **as your friend.**

MEMO NOTES

1.

2.

3.

4.

DECEMBER

12th

1. Is your marriage bed **kept sacred and pure?**

2. **Listen to your heart.** It is always asking for My help.

3. Be thankful in your heart for where you live and work, and for **friends and family** you have shared.

4. A **complainer** has little to share with others except themselves.

Memo Notes

1.

2.

3.

4.

DECEMBER

13ᵀᴴ

1. Live **your life for Me** as I live My life in you.

2. Anxiety may be a symptom of **your unbelief.**

3. **Do not worry** about anything, but pray about everything.

4. How many times will I tell you **I love you**? As many times as your heart opens to hear me.

Memo Notes

1.

2.

3.

4.

DECEMBER

14ᵀᴴ

1. **Stillness before Me.** Learn to live by it through life.

2. When you are at the **end of self**, let it be the beginning of Me.

3. **Major accident**, ignorance of my word.

4. Man did not put My thoughts into writing. Man only wrote what was **inspired** by the spirit from the Father's heart.

Memo Notes

1.

2.

3.

4.

DECEMBER

15TH

1. **Obey me:** Man does not like to be criticized, neither did my son for telling the truth.

2. **Bearing Godly fruit** in others is good fruit in the Father's eye.

3. Do not follow Me by self, but **by faith**.

4. Who is better to **instruct you** than the Father through the Holy Spirit.

MEMO NOTES

1.

2.

3.

4.

DECEMBER

16TH

1. It is important to view your life as I see it. It will **void your pathway** from more trials.

2. **Everything your heart** is lacking is everything I AM offering.

3. **Search for Me** until you meet Me face to face.

4. My children show Me **how much you love Me**. Follow My commandments and My law, and obey them always.

MEMO NOTES

1.

2.

3.

4.

DECEMBER

17TH

1. **When you tithe**, you are testing Me in your faith. I will bless you much more than just money.

2. Apart from Me you will not function in my **Father's wisdom**.

3. Prayer will **prevent you** from being discouraged.

4. **Partial obedience** is disobedience in the Father's eye.

MEMO NOTES

1.

2.

3.

4.

DECEMBER

18TH

1. It takes time to know Me child. Why not **start your watch** today?

2. A smile **costs less** than what you think.

3. Be a **shame of self** for not listening to what the Father has said.

4. **Rude parenting:** How ignorant that can be to My children.

MEMO NOTES

1.

2.

3.

4.

19ᵗʰ

1. Let me translate the Father's thoughts into your language. **He loves you.**

2. Man's heart can become like a clogged line **full of self** with no room for others.

3. I am not on a time schedule to listen to My children speak. I am **available always.**

4. **Reputation**: How will man remember yours?

Memo Notes

1.

2.

3.

4.

20TH

1. **Finding who you are.** How simple, **ask Me**.

2. Where in the world can you find Me? **Everywhere you seek.**

3. **Preparation Day:** Plan your life to continue tomorrow, but prepare your heart for my return this day.

4. Keep living your **life for Me**. It will never become boring.

MEMO NOTES

1.

2.

3.

4.

21ˢᵗ

1. If you **persevere My trials**, the Father will reward you greatly.

2. **My wisdom** is attainable, but does not come without asking.

3. **Man fighting with one another** will never save a life, only a relationship with my son, Jesus Christ.

4. Who knows more than the Father what tomorrow will bring? Have you **prepared your life** for his return?

Memo Notes

1.

2.

3.

4.

DECEMBER

22ND

1. **Thankfulness**: very meaningful word.

2. You listen to Me, my child. **How Important** that will become.

3. **Walk with Me** every day because that is who you are.

4. I say to you, the **beauty of your heart** is much richer than the clothes you wear, the car you drive, and where you live.

MEMO NOTES

1.

2.

3.

4.

DECEMBER

23ᴿᴰ

1. Nothing in your heart is **closer to the truth** than knowing Me.

2. You could never improve on **My timing.**

3. Where does kindness come from? I assure you **not from man's heart.**

4. So many of My children are headed in the **wrong direction.** So many have become lifers of wrong decisions.

Memo Notes

1.

2.

3.

4.

DECEMBER

24ᵀᴴ

1. **Deceiving a brother** to hurt his life is unacceptable.

2. A **silent Christian** is one not following my instruction.

3. My children, you have an ear to listen, a heart to obey. **Consider all a blessing.**

4. No one honors the Father more than **a doer of His Word.**

Memo Notes

1.

2.

3.

4.

DECEMBER

25TH

1. Let My Word be **your compass**.

2. **Heaven** or **Hell:** Man's death rate is 100 percent. Without me it remains the same.

3. **One who listens** to the Father reveals much in His heart.

4. **How much longer** shall I wait for My disobedient children to return.

———◆———

MEMO NOTES

1.

2.

3.

4.

DECEMBER

26ᵀᴴ

1. There is no place like home and there is no place like Heaven. **See my children soon.**

2. My book is finished, but your life has **just begun**.

3. No one speaks to the Father closer than me. Do you want to know **what He has to say?**

4. Are you hungry for eternal life, come **join Me in the Father's house.**

MEMO NOTES

1.

2.

3.

4.

DECEMBER

27ᵀᴴ

1. Share Me from your heart. Let none of My children **go unspoken** to.

2. Saddle up your bags and **pack your life** for a journey into my kingdom.

3. Is there anyone in your life that loves you more than the Father and me? Tell us, **we want to meet them.**

4. Your love for Me is different than the love of money. **Money satisfies for a season.** The Father's and Mine last for eternity.

MEMO NOTES

1.

2.

3.

4.

28ᵗʰ

1. **Read my words** with a pen or pencil in your hand.

2. Many of My children are afraid to surrender their lives to Me. **If they only knew** what they will be missing.

3. I can trust you, child, because you **believe in what I say**.

4. Are you a **listener of My Word** or ignoring me in your heart?

Memo Notes

1.

2.

3.

4.

DECEMBER

29TH

1. Many of my sheep know my voice but few **obey my calling.**

2. **Treasure book**: If you are looking for the truth outside my word, your filling the heart with man's lies.

3. What **I share** with man's Heart will **last forever.** What man shares with man will surely disappear.

4. You are the **Father's masterpiece** of his image.

MEMO NOTES

1.

2.

3.

4.

DECEMBER

30TH

1. Similarities: **You and Me.** How precious.

2. **Keep up with Me** in these days. My Word never becomes old.

3. It is no wonder many of My children do not know Me. They **spend little time** with me in the Father's word.

4. Finding yourself in darkness is easy if I am **leading your way**.

MEMO NOTES

1.

2.

3.

4.

31ST

1. When you pray to the Father, He allows Me to speak to your heart through **his Holy Spirit**.

2. Always share **your thankful** heart with others. It brings happiness into their lives.

3. What are My children searching for? Will this world satisfy your hungry heart? **You be the judge.**

4. The conclusion of My Word is My **children's wellness**.

Memo Notes

1.

2.

3.

4.

Lightning Source UK Ltd.
Milton Keynes UK
UKHW010655031120
372716UK00001B/17